ENGLISH

KEY STAGE TWO
SCOTTISH LEVELS C-E

DRAMA

LARRAINE S HARRISON

Published by Scholastic Ltd,
Villiers House,
Clarendon Avenue,
Leamington Spa,
Warwickshire CV32 5PR
Text © Larraine S Harrison
© 1999 Scholastic Ltd
2 3 4 5 6 7 8 9 0   1 2 3 4 5

AUTHOR
LARRAINE S HARRISON

EDITOR
CLARE GALLAHER

ASSISTANT EDITOR
CLARE MILLER

SERIES DESIGNER
LYNNE JOESBURY

DESIGNER
MARK UDALL

ILLUSTRATIONS
ROBIN LAWRIE

COVER ILLUSTRATION
JONATHAN BENTLEY

INFORMATION TECHNOLOGY CONSULTANT
MARTIN BLOWS

SCOTTISH 5–14 LINKS
MARGARET SCOTT AND SUSAN GOW

Designed using Adobe Pagemaker

British Library Cataloguing-in-Publication Data
A catalogue record for this book is available from the
British Library.

ISBN 0-590-53785-7

Contents

Introduction

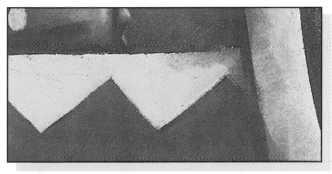

Scholastic Curriculum Bank is a series for all primary teachers, providing an essential planning tool for devising comprehensive schemes of work as well as an easily accessible and varied bank of practical, classroom-tested activities with photocopiable resources.

Designed to help planning for and implementation of progression, differentiation and assessment, *Scholastic Curriculum Bank* offers a structured range of stimulating activities with clearly stated learning objectives that reflect the programmes of study, and detailed lesson plans that allow busy teachers to put ideas into practice with the minimum amount of preparation time. The photocopiable sheets that accompany many of the activities provide ways of integrating purposeful application of knowledge and skills, differentiation, assessment and record-keeping.

Opportunities for formative assessment are highlighted within the activities where appropriate. Ways of using information technology for different purposes and in different contexts, as a tool for communicating and handling information and as a means of investigating, are integrated into the activities where appropriate, and more explicit guidance is provided at the end of the book.

The series covers all the primary curriculum subjects, with separate books for Key Stages 1 and 2 or Scottish Levels A–B and C–E. It can be used as a flexible resource with any scheme, to fulfil National Curriculum and Scottish 5–14 requirements and to provide children with a variety of different learning experiences that will lead to effective acquisition of skills and knowledge.

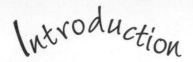
SCHOLASTIC CURRICULUM BANK ENGLISH

The *Scholastic Curriculum Bank English* books enable teachers to plan comprehensive and structured coverage of the primary English curriculum, and enable pupils to develop the required skills, knowledge and understanding through activities.

Each book contains one key stage. There are six books for Key Stage 1/Scottish levels A–B and six for Key Stage 2/Scottish levels C–E. These books reflect the English programme of study, so that there are titles on Reading, Writing, Speaking and listening and Spelling and phonics. The titles on Drama and Poetry cover all four aspects of the programme of study in relation to these subjects.

Bank of activities
This book provides a bank of activities which are designed to broaden children's experience of drama and enable them to develop their confidence and skill in working in drama.

Lesson plans
Detailed lesson plans, under clear headings, are given for each activity and provide material for immediate implementation in the classroom. The structure for each activity is as follows.

Activity title box
The information contained in the box at the beginning of each activity outlines the following key aspects:

▲ *Activity title and learning objective.* For each activity a clearly stated learning objective is given in bold italics. These learning objectives break down aspects of the programmes of study for English and The National Literacy Strategy's *Framework for Teaching* into manageable, hierarchical teaching and learning chunks, and their purpose is to aid planning for progression. These objectives can be linked to the National Curriculum and Scottish 5–14 requirements by referring to the overview grid at the end of this chapter (pages 9 to 12).

▲ *Class organization/Likely duration.* Icons ✝✝ and 🕐 signpost the suggested group sizes for each activity and the approximate amount of time required to complete it. Some activities are written to cover two or more sessions, and you may choose to extend other activities into more than one session if appropriate.

Previous skills/knowledge needed
Information is given here when it is necessary for the children to have acquired specific knowledge or skills prior to carrying out the activity.

Key background information
The information in this section outlines the main area of study and focuses on any particular teaching points that need to be addressed.

Preparation
Advice is given for those occasions when it is necessary for the teacher to carry out preparations for the activity. These often include preparing materials or making an appropriate setting for the drama.

Resources needed
All of the materials needed to carry out the activity are listed, so that the pupils or the teacher can gather them together easily before the beginning of the teaching session.

What to do
Easy-to-follow, step-by-step instructions are given for carrying out the activity, including suggestions for questions and discussion, as well as how to start and stop the drama when appropriate.

Suggestion(s) for extension/support
Ideas are given for ways of providing easy differentiation where activities lend themselves to this purpose. In all cases, suggestions are provided as to ways in which each activity can be modified for less able or extended for more able children.

Assessment opportunities
Where appropriate, opportunities for ongoing teacher assessment of the children's work during or after a specific activity are highlighted.

Opportunities for IT
Where opportunities for IT present themselves, these are briefly outlined with reference to particularly suitable types of program. The chart on page 159 presents specific areas of IT covered in the activities, together with more detailed support on how to apply particular types of program. Selected lesson plans serve as models for other activities by providing more comprehensive guidance on the

application of IT; these lesson plans are indicated by bold page numbers on the grid and the ◈ icon at the start of an activity.

Performance ideas

For many drama activities, a performance is an appropriate outcome rather than (or as well as) a display. In these cases, a range of performance activities are suggested, often based on the previous drama work that has been done.

Display ideas

Where they are relevant and innovative, display ideas are incorporated into activity plans and illustrated with examples.

Reference to photocopiable sheets

Where activities include photocopiable activity sheets, small reproductions of these are included in the lesson plans together with guidance notes for their use.

Assessment

Children's development in drama will take place over time, as they become more familiar and more confident in the medium. Progress is often more spiral than linear, as drama strategies are revisited and extended through the key stages. Drama also has many forms and this makes drama difficult to assess. It is therefore important for the teacher to be clear about exactly what aspect of drama is being assessed at any one time. An ability to co-operate and take part fully in a whole group role-play demands different skills from devising and performing in groups. There are social skills as well as drama and theatre skills involved and sometimes these processes overlap in one activity. Drama affords an opportunity for holistic learning which is difficult to quantify.

However, some assessment in drama is possible and one should look for ways to categorize the learning in order to make these assessments. There are several possibilities, but one way is to divide drama into three broad categories: devising, performing and spontaneous role-play. Within these three categories there are many subdivisions. The following list provides some examples.

▲ Devising skills: the ability to shape the material and plan and predict outcomes; to contribute ideas and develop the ideas of others; to negotiate; to recognize problems and consider the effectiveness of different styles of presentation.

▲ Performance skills: the ability to communicate effectively and imaginatively in role through speech and movement; to evaluate a piece of drama using appropriate theatre vocabulary.

▲ Spontaneous role-play: the ability to respond appropriately in role; to identify implications within the role-play; to initiate and sustain a line of thought in relation to the content of the drama; to have confidence in using and responding to a variety of different drama strategies; to understand and use symbolic representations in drama.

Photocopiable sheets

Many of the activities are accompanied by photocopiable sheets. Drama is essentially a practical subject, but there are many occasions when a photocopiable sheet can be used to prepare for an activity or to focus on an aspect of the work during the drama or as a conclusion. Other sheets are intended to be used as a resource for the teacher to use in connection with specific activities. The sheets provide purposeful activities that are ideal for assessment and can be kept as records in pupils' portfolios of work.

Cross-curricular links

Cross-curricular links are identified on a simple grid which cross-references the particular areas of study in English to the programmes of study for other subjects in the curriculum (see page 160).

DRAMA

Drama is an active way of learning and feeds into many areas of the Key Stage 2 curriculum. It works on intellectual, aesthetic and emotional levels to provide a powerful and effective way of learning, as well as being an art form in its own right. The four chapters in this book reflect this diversity by offering activities under the headings of Language and Literacy, Theatre Skills, Personal and Social Development, and Cross-curricular Themes.

Drama can be a challenging subject to teach and many teachers lack confidence and experience in this area. Some teachers also fear losing control in what is often perceived to be a laissez-faire activity. The drama activities in this book are carefully structured to encourage an enjoyable but disciplined approach to drama, and many are suited to the more cautious teacher working with an inexperienced class. However, this book also provides ideas which include strategies for the more confident teacher. Limited time for hall space is another common problem for drama. With this in mind, many of the activities have been designed to take place in the classroom, often without the need to rearrange all the furniture.

Drama provides an alternative way of learning, which can be planned in as part of the methodology for teaching English and other aspects of the National Curriculum. Drama strategies such as freeze-frames and other active learning methods are particularly useful for shared reading during the Literacy Hour. Children can also work independently on script writing and on writing within imaginary contexts of drama where appropriate. However, drama should also be included with art, music and dance as part of the school's overall provision for the arts. The chapter on theatre skills is designed to accommodate this and concentrates on building up children's confidence and skill in this important curriculum area.

Most of the activities in this book are introduced according to a common pattern which underpins and supports the ensuing work. The pattern follows three principles: making a contract, defining the space, and providing clear signs for starting and stopping.

Making a contract

This involves making an agreement with the children that they will accept the imaginary context and behave accordingly for the duration of the drama. Phrases associated with the media can often be employed to explain what is required, such as 'taking part in a reconstruction of an event' or 'making a story for an imaginary video'. Whatever the context, the children are usually asked to play the parts of different people who are often in a different place and sometimes even in a different time. The contract need not be formal or lengthy and should be spoken with the expectation that the children will agree and that they will enjoy the drama.

Making the contract is important for a number of reasons. It means that if a child breaks the contract by behaving inappropriately in the drama, he or she risks being excluded from the action. In the majority of cases this will not be necessary, as a reminder of the contract will be all that is needed. If a child will not agree to enter into the contract, he or she should be offered alternative work to complete at the side of the room.

Defining the space

Children need to be clear about what is to be used in the drama and what isn't. With inexperienced children or a new space, mention all the areas and equipment that are out of bounds for the duration of the drama, for example PE equipment and music trolleys. If children ignore this, then stop the drama and remind them of the boundaries.

The majority of children enjoy drama and will readily agree to the rules to make the drama succeed.

Clear signs for starting and stopping

Children need to know when the drama is starting and when they are to stop. It is also important for the teacher to be able to stop the drama quickly if necessary. Most activities use the word 'Action' to start the drama and the word 'Freeze' to stop. The word 'Freeze' is sometimes preceded by, or replaced by, the blowing of a whistle, if the activity is noisy and the children would find it difficult to hear. The children should always be told what method will be used.

When an activity involves the teacher taking on a role, a clear sign of role should be used, so that the children know when the teacher is in role and when he or she is not. Visual signs such as wearing a piece of clothing or carrying a small item such as a clipboard are often best, but any sign can be used as long as it is clear.

Props and equipment

Excessive use of props can often distract children from the main focus of the drama and it is often better to ask the children to mime what they need. However, a few carefully chosen props can be very effective and the same props can often be used to represent a variety of things. Simple props and costumes are more versatile than elaborate ones. The following items are among the most useful: cloaks, waistcoats, bags, sticks, interesting pictures or maps, unusual objects and precious-looking objects such as a silver cup or bowl, a clipboard, a bunch of keys, historical artefacts, a crown; lengths of material are very versatile and can be draped over tables and chairs or put on PE mats to represent a river or pond; percussion instruments can also provide support for drama, and a cassette player and audio cassettes can be used to create atmosphere or record children in action.

Drama can often take place successfully in the classroom but some activities need a large space such as a hall. When working in a large space try to make it as free from interruption as possible, within the confines of the building. A few chairs and a small table are often useful for defining imaginary places or providing a visual focus. If small drama blocks are available they can be used to provide different levels when making dramatic environments. Lighting is rarely an option for primary schools, apart from special occasions such as the school play, but if it is available it can be used to good effect to create atmosphere or create areas of light and darkness to represent imaginary places.

Learning objective	PoS/AO	Content	Type of activity	Page
Language and literacy				
To develop the use of physical theatre in relation to written symbols.	Sp & List: 1d. Writing: 2c. **English Language 5–14** *Knowledge about language: Level C.*	Making punctuation marks with body shapes and movement.	Whole class, with children using their bodies to create different shapes. Groups performing moves to add punctuation to word cards.	14
To build confidence in devising and performing small group improvisations.	Sp & List: 1d. Writing: 3b. *As above.*	Devising and performing, using specified parts of speech in a given context.	Small groups devising improvisations to perform to whole class.	16
To use freeze-frames, spoken thoughts and forum theatre to explore texts from a number of different perspectives.	Sp & List: 1d. Reading: 2b. *Talking about texts: Level C.*	Discussing possible interpretations of text and making depictions.	Whole-class discussion of a freeze-frame. Small groups performing to whole class.	18
To develop confidence in presenting a point of view in role.	Sp & List: 1a, b, c, d; 2a, b. *As above.*	Taking part as experts in an imaginary radio discussion programme.	Preparing an argument in pairs, followed by whole-class discussion.	20
To use role-play to devise and perform stories for a specified audience.	Sp & List: 1a, b, d. *Imaginative writing: Level C.*	Creating, performing and writing a class story for imaginary audiences.	Whole class brainstorming the beginning and end of a class story. Small groups work out events for the middle of the story.	22
To develop skills in devising and performing plays for a specific audience.	Sp & List: 1a, b, d Writing: 1b, c. *Audience awareness: Level C.*	Performing a story for younger children and adapting it for older children.	Whole class mime the main events of a fairy tale. Small groups work out a scene for a modern version of the tale.	24
To build confidence in developing a story, using a range of drama strategies.	Sp & List: 1a, d; 2a, b. *Talking in groups: Level D.*	Working in and out of role to develop the story of a search for a mysterious person.	Whole class working in role as a community, then acting out the next part of the story after discussion.	26
To use physical theatre and spoken thoughts to create a character and stimulate improvisation.	Sp & List: 1d *Talking about experiences, feelings and opinions: Level C.*	Making a pathway for a character and inventing flashbacks about the character's life and thoughts.	Whole class improvising a suitable situation, then small groups making freeze-frames of alternative events.	29
To use role-play and whole-group drama to create an opportunity for recall and reflection on a story.	Sp & List: 1a, d; 2a. Reading: 1d. *Talking about texts: Level C.*	Taking part in interviews and making a commemorative garden for a character in a story.	Whole class deciding on a garden. Pairs interviewing each other as police and reporters.	32
To develop confidence in using hot-seating to explore perspectives on literary texts.	Sp & List: 1d, 2b. Writing: 1a, b. *Talking about experiences, feelings and opinions: Level C.*	Taking on the roles of characters to answer questions about feelings and relationships.	Whole class questioning a group who speak on behalf of a character. Pairs devising questions and then becoming other characters in the story.	34
Theatre skills				
To develop skills in the writing and performance of scripted drama.	Sp & List: 1a, d. Writing: 1b, c; 2b. **Expressive Arts 5–14** *Using language: Level D.*	Writing a script and reading it onto an audio cassette.	Small groups writing scripts and recording them in front of the whole class.	38

Learning objective	PoS/AO	Content	Type of activity	Page
To build confidence in the use of mime in performance.	Sp & List: 1d. *Using movement and mime: Level C.*	Taking part in exercises and short scenes involving mime.	Whole class and pairs taking part in mime exercises from cards.	42
To use actions to perform key words or phrases in a poem.	Sp & List: 1d. Reading: 1d, 2b. *As above.*	Inventing actions to communicate the meanings of key words or phrases in a poem.	Whole class suggesting mimes. Pairs working out and performing words from the poem.	43
To develop skills in devising, performing and evaluating a piece of drama.	Sp & List: 1a, d. Writing: 1b. *Evaluating and appreciating: Level C.*	Improvising and evaluating scenes based on conversations in a queue.	Small groups devising scenes and performing them to the whole class.	45
To use a picture as a stimulus for small group improvisations.	Sp & List: 1a, d. *Expressing thoughts and ideas: Level C.*	Playing the people in a painting, who come alive for one minute.	Small groups depicting a painting and performing it to the whole class.	47
To create small group improvisations from a given first line.	Sp & List: 1a, d. *Using language: Level D.*	Devising and performing improvisations based on given first lines.	Small groups devising improvisations to perform to whole class.	49
To develop confidence in starting an improvisation with a non-verbal activity.	Sp & List: 1a, d. *Using movement and mime: Level C.*	Playing and re-playing the first minute of a scene using silent entrances.	Small groups working out mimes and performing them to the whole class.	50
To give children an opportunity to perform in the style of television or radio advertising.	Sp & List: 1a, d; 3b. *Expressing, communicating and presenting: Level D.*	Performing imaginary TV or radio adverts, using appropriate language and mannerisms.	Small groups devising adverts for new inventions based on slogans, and performing them to the whole class.	52
To build confidence in performing a play in front of a larger audience.	Sp & List: 1a, d. Reading: 1a; 2b. *As above.*	Exploring events, characters and themes within a play and performing with an awareness of audience.	Whole class and small groups doing exercises to improve their skills of interpretation and performance.	54
To encourage children to make constructive responses to drama they have watched.	Sp & List: 1a, d; 2a. *Evaluating and appreciating: Level D.*	Thinking about specific aspects of drama performances.	Whole class and small groups discussing and constructively criticising performances.	58
Personal and social development				
To use hot-seating and role-play to stimulate discussion and debate.	Sp & List: 1a, d; 2a, b. **Religious and Moral Education** *Relationships and moral values: Level D.*	Taking part in an imaginary TV debate.	Whole class considering various points of view on a domestic incident. One group role-playing characters with other groups preparing and asking questions.	62
To use issues of social debate to stimulate argument in small group improvisations.	Sp & List: 1a, d; 2b. Writing: 1a, c. *Personal and social development.*	Improvising an argument about censorship of videos.	Whole class and small groups discussing issues of censorship and improvising arguments on the issue based on a given incident.	63

DRAMA

Learning objective	PoS/AO	Content	Type of activity	Page
To build children's confidence in using spontaneous improvisation and creating situations for drama.	Sp & List: 1a, d; 2a, b. *As above.*	Using drama strategies to explore events and feelings surrounding an imaginary bullying incident.	Pairs defining what constitutes bullying. Whole class discussing an invented bullying incident.	65
To use an everyday problem as a focus for a variety of drama strategies.	Sp & List: 1a, d. Writing: 1c. *As above.*	Playing the parts of people who work on a magazine's problem page.	Whole class and/or pairs exploring an imaginary problem.	67
To extend children's understanding of still image towards a more symbolic dimension.	Sp & List: 1a, d. *As above.*	Making imaginary sculptures and improvisations about friends and enemies.	Whole class exploring ways to symbolize feelings. Pairs working to create a group sculpture.	69
To give children roles of responsibility within a whole-group drama.	Sp & List: 1a, d; 2a, b. Writing: 1a, b, c. ***Environmental Studies*** *People in society: Level D. PSD.*	Designing and running an imaginary health and fitness centre.	Whole class and small groups using mime, improvisation and discussion to create and solve problems within the imaginary context.	71
To use an issue as a focus for developing a whole-group drama experience.	Sp & List: 1a, d; 2a. Writing: 2a. ***Religious and Moral Education*** *Relationships and moral values: Level D.*	Taking on the roles of evacuees from an imaginary volcanic island who become the victims of prejudice.	Pairs and groups working out mimes. Whole class improvising as a community and discussing and recording their responses in writing.	74
To use a topical issue as a focus for developing whole-group drama.	Sp & List: 1a, d; 2a, b. ***Environmental Studies*** *People in society. Developing informed attitudes: Level D.*	Taking on the roles of circus workers who use animals.	Whole class and small groups taking part in improvisation and discussion in and out of role.	78
To develop children's confidence in solving problems and negotiating decisions in role.	Sp & List: 1a, d, 2a, b. Writing: 1b. *As above.*	Taking on the roles of new settlers making new laws.	Whole class, pairs and small groups improvising and making decisions in role.	82
To use drama games to develop social skills to support ongoing work in drama.	Sp & List: 1d. ***Expressive Arts 5–14*** *Drama. Communicating: Level C/D.*	Playing drama games.	Whole class and pairs taking part in a variety of games involving physical and mental activities.	84
Cross-curricular themes				
To build confidence in playing roles within a whole-group historical context.	Sp & List: 1d. Reading: 1b/2c. Writing: 1a, b. ***Environmental Studies*** *Social subjects. People in the past: Level C.*	Taking on the roles of villagers in a historical period.	Whole class and groups re-creating a version of a historical community and solving problems in role.	88

Learning objective	PoS/AO	Content	Type of activity	Page
To re-enact aspects of a historical event from the perspective of participants.	Sp & List: 1d. Writing: 1b. *As above, Level D.*	Re-enacting the discovery of the tomb of Tutankhamun.	Whole class and groups re-enacting parts of a story.	91
To re-enact parts of a myth using whole-group drama, freeze-frames and spoken thoughts.	Sp & List: 1a, d. Writing: 1a, b. *As above, Level C.*	Re-enacting parts of the story of Theseus and the Minotaur.	Whole class, pairs and groups using movement and mime with some discussion in role.	95
To increase an understanding of historical events through role-play and teacher-in-role.	Sp & List: 1a, d; 2b. *As above, Level C.*	Discussing Celtic responses while in role as Roman soldiers.	Pairs, working in groups, hearing viewpoints from the perspective of Roman soldiers building a road.	98
To build confidence in using persuasive vocabulary and images within a dramatic context.	Sp & List: 1a, d. *As above, Level D.*	Taking part in an imaginary TV show about the local area.	Whole class and groups considering how best to 'sell' their local area.	100
To build confidence in playing two opposing roles within the same dramatic context.	Sp & List: 1a, d; 2a, b. *Social subjects. People in society: Level D.*	Taking on roles as villagers and theme park developers.	Whole class and small groups moving between two opposing sides to improvise an environmental conflict.	102
To encourage roles of responsibility and problem-solving within a whole-group drama.	Sp & List: 1a, d. Writing: 1b. *As above, Level D.*	Designing and working on an imaginary campsite.	Whole class and small groups using mime and improvisation to explore issues on a campsite.	108
To build confidence in moving from sound and movement to improvisation.	Sp & List: 1a, d. Writing: 1b. *People and places: Level A/B.*	Moving and making sounds as factory machines and playing the parts of factory workers.	Whole class and pairs using movement, sound and improvisation.	111
To develop skills in using physical theatre to represent two-dimensional shapes.	Sp & List: 1d. **Mathematics 5–14** *Number, money, measure: Level B.*	Using body shapes to make numbers and sums.	Whole class and pairs using their bodies to make numbers and record sums.	113

Entries given in italics relate to the following Scottish National guidelines: English Language 5–14, Expressive Arts 5–14, Religious and Moral Education, Environmental Studies and Mathematics 5–14.

Language and literacy

Drama is a powerful and effective means through which to teach aspects of language and literacy. It provides a range of imaginary audiences for speaking and listening and for writing and can bring aspects of a text to life for closer analysis and reflection. Through the methods suggested in this chapter, the deeper meanings of a text can be brought to the surface as the children explore moments from the different perspectives of the characters and create their own image of the events. When drama is used in this way, it gives clear messages to children that literature is open to interpretation and has layers of meaning beyond the literal.

This chapter suggests ways in which aspects of punctuation and grammar can be enlivened through drama to facilitate greater understanding and support more formal work. Creative writing is also stimulated and supported when children are allowed to experience a story in drama before being asked to write.

Speaking and listening is crucial in the drive to improve literacy, and this chapter contains many activities to support and extend children's language. For example, children are given roles as experts to encourage them to explain and justify their opinions within a context that raises their self-esteem. Whole-group drama encourages them to adopt the language of negotiation and debate in contexts that would not be possible in real life. A range of contexts for language development are provided, which will help to support ongoing attempts to improve children's literacy.

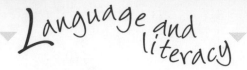

PUNCTUATION LINE UP

To develop the use of physical theatre in relation to written symbols.

†† *Whole class.*

🕐 *Session One: 10 minutes. Session Two: 30 minutes.*

Previous skills/knowledge needed

The children will need some knowledge of basic punctuation marks.

Key background information

This activity is intended to support and reinforce ongoing work on basic punctuation by using physical theatre to depict the shapes of the punctuation marks. The work is divided into two sessions which can be completed in one lesson or spread over two lessons. Session One links specific movements with punctuation marks and requires a hall in which the activity can be carried out. Session Two, which takes place in the classroom, can be repeated using different words on subsequent occasions.

Preparation

Make one copy per child of photocopiable page 116. Prepare 11 large word cards: I / hate / toast / said / Jo / shouted / Do / you / like / asked / Sam.

Resources needed

A large space, photocopiable page 116, 11 word cards (see 'Preparation'), writing materials.

opening speech marks

closing speech marks

question mark (and one jump for dot)

exclamation mark (and one jump for dot)

What to do

Session One

In the hall, tell the children to find a space. Explain that when you say 'Go' they should walk around the room in any direction, without touching anyone else. When you say the words 'Full stop', they should stamp their feet and stop. On the word 'Go' they should set off again, but if you say the word 'Comma', they must pause to take a diagonal step. Then they can carry on walking until you say 'Full stop', as before. Each time the children set off, add another punctuation movement to the ones that you have already used, varying them to make it seem like a game.

Other movements include the following:

▲ *Opening speech marks* – pause and arch two arms forward to make the shape of inverted commas before moving on.

▲ *Closing speech marks* – stop, turn around 180 degrees and make the same shape as above but in the opposite direction. Wait for the word 'Go' before moving on.

▲ *Question mark* – stop, make the shape of the arched part of the question mark by curving the arms above the head, with the body representing the stick, then give a jump with both feet to represent the dot underneath. Wait for the word 'Go' before moving on.

▲ *Exclamation mark* – stop, put the hands together and put both arms straight up in the air. Give a jump with both feet to represent the dot underneath. Wait for the word 'Go' before moving on.

Session Two

Ask the children to sit down, and clear a space at the front of the classroom which everyone can see. Choose five children and give each child one of the following word cards: I / hate / toast / said / Jo.

Ask the five children to stand at the front of the classroom and make the words into a sentence by holding them in front of their bodies at waist height. Explain that each child should say the word on their card as you point to it. Point to the words in turn, making a sentence. Ask the class to tell you what would be missing if these words were written in a book. Whatever punctuation is suggested, ask the child who made the suggestion to stand at the front, in the place where the mark would be in the sentence. For example, the full stop would stand after the word card 'Jo'.

Continue until all the necessary punctuation has been represented by children from the class, to form a 'Punctuation line up'. Explain that when you point to the children representing punctuation marks, they should make a static version of the appropriate movement. The comma must take one step diagonally, the opening and closing speech marks must move their arms the correct way and the full stop must stamp one foot. Now point to each child in turn and let them respond with a movement or a word in order to perform the sentence.

Next, replace the word 'said' with the word 'shouted' and ask the class if this changes anything. An exclamation mark can be added and the comma removed. Discuss how the exclamation mark will affect the way the words in between the speech marks are spoken. Now perform this new version of the sentence, with the direct speech being shouted.

Ask these children to sit down, and choose some more children to hold up the words: Do / you / like / toast / asked / Sam. Add the correct punctuation to this sentence, using movements as before.

Give out copies of photocopiable page 116. Ask the children to complete the sheet individually, before working in pairs or threes to work out a sound for each punctuation mark. (Emphasize that only tasteful sounds will be acceptable.) Ask each group to choose one of the sentences on the sheet to read out with their punctuation sounds.

Finally, perform the two original sentences again, but this time ask the children representing the punctuation to make a sound to accompany their movements.

This activity can be repeated on subsequent occasions using different sentences.

Suggestion(s) for extension

Give groups of children some reading material and tell them to look for a sentence containing several punctuation marks. Ask them to copy out the sentence with the correct punctuation and then write each word on a separate piece of A4 paper. Groups can give these word papers to the class to see if they can perform the sentence with the correct punctuation.

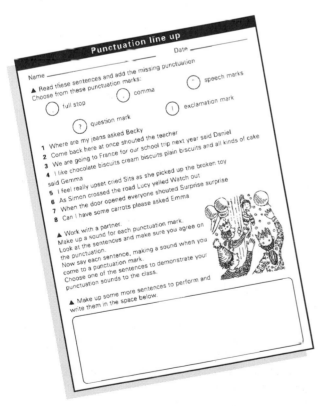

Suggestion(s) for support

Make cards with punctuation marks on them (one punctuation mark for each card) and ask some children to hold up the correct punctuation card behind those making the movements and sounds. Complete a copy of photocopiable page 116 as a whole class and make a class decision on which sounds to use.

Assessment opportunities

This activity provides a good opportunity to assess the children's understanding of basic punctuation marks and where they should be placed in a sentence. It also reveals children's confidence in using their bodies to make and perform different shapes.

Opportunities for IT

Let pairs of children record different sentences onto an audio cassette, using their own sounds for the punctuation. Ask the class to listen to the tape to guess which sounds represent which punctuation marks each time.

Performance ideas

A 'Punctuation line up', as described in Session Two, can be turned into a class performance by lengthening the sentence, so that all the class is involved. The long line can be accommodated around the perimeter of the room, to create a performance, with the audience in the middle.

Reference to photocopiable sheet

Photocopiable page 116 provides a punctuation exercise as well as an opportunity for the children to add their own interpretations to the punctuation movements by inventing and performing accompanying sounds. Children are also invited to invent some sentences of their own to perform as a punctuation line up.

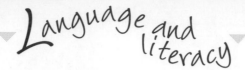

THE GRAMMAR WAITING ROOM

To build confidence in devising and performing small group improvisations.

†† *Small groups performing to the whole class.*

🕐 *45–60 minutes.*

Previous skills/knowledge needed

Children should have some awareness of the function of nouns, verbs or adjectives in a sentence.

Key background information

The tightly structured framework of this activity is designed to support children who are cautious of devising and performing drama in small groups. However, the structure also enables more confident children to focus on the quality of their contributions rather than on the quantity. It seeks to establish clear guidelines to facilitate improvisation work in the future. The subject matter also provides an opportunity for the children to focus on using parts of speech in a life-like context. This activity provides an introduction to the freeze command, which can be used as a stopping signal during other drama activities.

Preparation

Clear an acting area at the front of the classroom and place four chairs in a line facing the audience. Select which part of speech you wish to focus on (nouns, verbs or adjectives) and decide on a type of waiting room for the improvisation. Fold a piece of card so that it will stand up. Make the card into a sign, to indicate the type of waiting room you have selected, such as 'Filler's Dental Surgery', 'Doctor's Surgery. Please Wait Here' or 'Short Cut Hairdressing Salon'.

Fold six pieces of card so that they will stand up. Use these to make six word cards relating to either nouns, verbs or adjectives. The words should have some connection with the context. For example:

▲ *Noun cards* in a dentist's waiting room might include tooth / chair / injection / Ben / Mr Jones / November.

▲ *Verb cards* in a doctor's waiting room might include different forms of a verb on each card such as hurt, hurts, hurting / wait, waits, waited, waiting / ache, aches, ached, aching / feel, feels, felt, feeling / walk, walks, walked, walking / work, works, worked, working.

▲ *Adjective cards* in a hairdresser's waiting room might include spiky / blonde / frizzy / expensive / silly / beautiful.

Resources needed

An acting area and six chairs, cards (see 'Preparation').

What to do

Put the waiting room sign on a chair at one end of the acting area. Organize the class into groups of four. Ask one group to sit on the chairs in the acting area. Use this group to help you explain the task. Ask the children to imagine that the acting area is a waiting room and that the people on the chairs are waiting. Give the children one card each and explain that when the improvisation starts, the person sitting in the first chair will be the first person to speak. This person must start a conversation with the others that contains the word on his or her card. (For example, in a dentist's waiting room, the first person would have to say something with the word 'tooth' in it.) Ask the class for suggestions and let the child in the first chair select a sentence from the suggestions offered.

Explain that the person in the second chair must now respond to this sentence but their response should contain the word on their card. Ask the class for suggestions. This pattern is repeated with the third and then the fourth child making a comment containing the word on their card.

If you are using verb cards, the children should choose just one of the verb forms on each card. Emphasize that the conversation must make sense in the context of the waiting room. If groups have enough time, they should carry on the conversation to include the unused fifth and sixth word card(s).

Ask the children at the front to place their cards on their chairs before leaving the acting area. Ask each group to number themselves 1 to 4 within their group. Then allocate one word card to each number, so that every child knows what their word is to be. Tell the children to use the same order as the order that was used on the chairs.

Explain to the children that they will be performing an improvisation working in their groups and incorporating the words that they have been given. Before asking the children to prepare their improvisations, explain that they should observe the following rules:

▲ The improvisation should last no longer than one minute for each group.

▲ In the interests of safety, the improvisation should not include any physical contact such as pushing or hitting nor any physical acts such as falling or jumping.

▲ Children are allowed to say what they want to say, as long as it fits into the scene and is not rude or silly.

▲ The improvisation should start with the first person in the group saying 'Action' and should finish with the last person to speak saying 'Freeze'. At this point the group should freeze for three seconds before relaxing.

The children can practise the improvisation sitting in groups in the classroom. They do not need to put their chairs in a line to rehearse. Give the children a rough idea of how long they have to practise (about ten to fifteen minutes) and then move around the groups to support and extend the work where necessary. Encourage fast workers to go back and look for ways to make their conversations more interesting. Ensure that every group has something that they can realistically perform, even if it is only a few words each.

Stop the groups and explain that when you give a signal, every group should start a final rehearsal of their improvisation. Let the groups rehearse simultaneously. When a group finishes, they should wait in silence for any groups who have yet to finish. Explain that you will stop the rehearsal after one more minute.

Now put the word cards on view on a table and let each group perform their improvisation to the class, using the four chairs at the front of the room. Encourage the actors to speak loud enough for everyone to hear but be careful not to embarrass children by stopping the action to draw attention to any one child. Ask the audience to check that all the word cards have been used. Insist that each performance is watched in silence, so that the actors can concentrate on their lines. Giving the children a round of applause and a few positive comments at the end of each improvisation will build up their confidence for future work of this kind.

Suggestion(s) for extension

Encourage the children to extend their conversations to one and a half or two minutes. Suggest that they include humour or tension, such as a joke or a problem, to sustain interest and maintain their focus.

Suggestion(s) for support

Encourage the children to work out very short sentences that they know they will remember. Let them write out their sentences for you, so that you can prompt them during their performance. Let children work as two sets of pairs in the waiting room.

Assessment opportunities

Note the children's ability to use extended sentences and imaginative language in their improvisations. Note also children's social skills in working with others in a creative context. Look for children who are able to express themselves confidently and clearly in performance and who attempt some kind of characterization within the role.

Opportunities for IT

Each group could write their lines as a script, using a word processor. They may need to be shown how to set out their work in the style of a script, separating the names of the speakers from the words that are spoken. This can be achieved in several ways depending on the software used.

If the children are using a standard word processor they will need to be shown how to use indents and tabs to create two columns of text. This can be done using hanging indents where the speech wraps around at the end of the line and comes back to the start of the speech line rather than to the left-hand margin of the page. This effect is usually achieved by adjusting the two left-hand margin markers on the ruler bar.

SARAH: *(Holding hands to mouth)* I've come because my front tooth is hurting so badly that I can hardly open my mouth.

BALPINDER: I hope the dentist won't decide to pull it out without giving you an injection to deaden the pain *(pretends to give an injection).*

Stage directions can be included in brackets and highlighted using italics.

If the children are using a frame-based word processor or a simple desktop publishing package, they can create two columns and type their text into the columns. In the example below, the frame borders are shown to highlight their position, but they can be turned off prior to the work being printed. In this format the text will automatically wrap around the end of the line to the start of the frame.

| Wayne | I washed my hair last night in the wrong shampoo and it's gone all spiky this morning. I hope the hairdresser can cut the spiky bits off. |
| Rachel | I'm going to ask the hairdresser to dye my hair blonde. |

More sophisticated word processors may allow children to set up a table which can be used in the same way as a frame. In this case, set up a three-column table so that there is a gap between the speaker's name and the words spoken. Table borders can be turned off so that they don't print on the page.

Speaker's name		speech

Performance ideas
Let each group perform another group's work, using the scripts (see 'Opportunities for IT').

Display ideas
Groups can draw cartoon versions of a moment from their improvisation using speech bubbles and these can be used as a display.

SIGNIFICANT MOMENTS

To use freeze-frames, spoken thoughts and forum theatre to explore texts from a number of different perspectives.

†† *Whole class directing small groups.*

⏱ *30 minutes.*

Previous skills/knowledge needed
Children will need to have an understanding of the text from which the chosen moment(s) have been taken.

Key background information
This activity involves a significant moment from a text being represented in a freeze-frame, in which a group of children represent the characters in a 'frozen' depiction of the moment. They are then asked to speak out an appropriate thought for each character. The class – that is, the forum – make key decisions about the freeze-frame and offer suggestions for the spoken thoughts. This activity provides a visual focus for reflection and analysis in relation to key moments in a text such as a novel, poem or play. It gives important messages to children that texts can be interpreted in a number of different ways, all of which are acceptable, providing they do not contradict the text. It encourages children to consider stories from a variety of perspectives, with particular regard to the characters' thoughts and feelings.

Preparation

Draw and cut out an A4-sized thought bubble from a piece of card. Select up to three significant moments from a text that have potential for discussion and analysis. Prepare appropriate questions about the moment to be depicted. Clear a small space for an acting area in the classroom.

Resources needed

Chosen text, thought bubbles (see 'Preparation').

What to do

Draw the children's attention to the moment in the text that you have chosen to focus on.

Arrange the class so that everyone can see the acting area. Ask the children to imagine that someone who was watching a video of the chosen text decided to pause it at a selected moment to make a freeze-frame. Explain that you would like the class to make a reconstruction of the freeze-frame based on a particular moment in the text that you have selected.

After a brief class discussion of your chosen moment from the text, choose a group of children to represent the characters in the freeze-frame. Ask these children to stand at the front. They should wait for the class to tell them how to make the freeze-frame. (If there are major disagreements on any aspect of the freeze-frame, other versions of the freeze-frame can be made later to accommodate the alternatives.) Start by asking the class where each of the characters should be positioned and where they should be looking. Invite the children to give reasons for their answers and relate the comments back to the text. Consider all feasible suggestions before deciding on the version for the freeze-frame.

Now make a practice freeze frame to see the effect. During this practice freeze-frame, hold the thought bubble over the head of each of the characters in turn and ask the

class what they think each character might be thinking. Encourage the children to give the exact words, as if the characters were thinking out loud. Explain that each character will be asked to speak out a thought during the final freeze-frame. Try to collect a number of different thoughts for each character and ask the children to justify their suggestions. The child playing the character should be given the final say on which thought to speak out loud during the freeze-frame. Encourage children to choose something they can remember. When the thoughts have been decided, ask each character to practise saying their thought aloud.

Explain the following procedure before completing the final freeze-frame with the spoken thoughts:
▲ On the word 'Freeze', the group must make the freeze-frame as agreed.
▲ On the word 'Thoughts', the characters must speak out their thoughts in a previously agreed order as they hold the 'frozen' positions.
▲ On the word 'Relax', after the last thought has been given, the group must break the freeze.

Repeat the above sequence to illustrate two more significant moments from the same text. Use different groups for each moment, if possible.

Suggestion(s) for extension

If the class is confident, organize them into small groups and ask each group to select an important and/or exciting moment from the text. Each group should work out and practise how to represent their moment in a freeze-frame, with thoughts. When completed, the freeze-frames can be performed to the rest of the class. Every child should be given the chance to take part in the freeze-frame. If there are insufficient characters for the group, some children can speak a thought for one of the characters (see 'Suggestion(s) for support') or it may be possible to invent more characters, such as onlookers or passers-by. More confident groups can be asked to bring their freeze-frames to life for up to half a minute, to include improvised direct speech, before finishing with another freeze-frame.

Suggestion(s) for support

Allow less confident children to use other children to speak out their character's thoughts on their behalf during the freeze-frame. Children acting as 'voices' should stand upright behind their characters during the freeze, to make it clear that they are not part of the visual representation. Ideally, the child representing the character should be in agreement with the thought spoken by his or her 'voice'.

Assessment opportunities

This activity provides an opportunity to assess children's ability to see beyond the literal interpretations of a text. Children's comments will reveal their ability to empathize

with the characters and their ability to identify underlying themes and issues. Children's suggestions for spoken thoughts will also indicate their ability to translate their ideas into the first person singular form of speech.

Opportunities for IT

If the school has access to a digital camera, or can scan photographs taken of the freeze-frames, the children can use these digitized pictures within a word processor or drawing package and add thought bubbles for each person.

A more ambitious project would be to use a multimedia authoring package which uses the pictures and the children's own voices (recorded using a microphone attached to the computer) to give their thoughts. If several freeze-frames are worked on, these could be put together in the same presentation to create a series of freeze frames.

Performance ideas

Perform the freeze-frames to a wider audience using a few props and costumes. Link the freeze-frames together with a narration, stopping at appropriate moments to perform the freeze-frames with thoughts. If appropriate, the freeze-frames can be brought to life for a few seconds to allow the characters to converse, before freezing again.

Display ideas

Take photographs of the freeze-frames or ask children to draw them. Stick handwritten thought bubbles onto the photographs or write thought bubbles onto the drawings. Display these with supporting pieces of the text to explain the significant moments.

PEOPLE MEET PEOPLE

To develop confidence in presenting a point of view in role.

†† *Whole class and pairs.*

⏱ *45–60 minutes.*

Previous skills/knowledge needed

Children need background information or knowledge of real-life news items relevant to the topic under discussion. A debate on land use, for example, might relate to some recent news items on the subject.

Key background information

This activity can be used with any current issue or debate which involves two opposing points of view. The issues can be of a domestic nature such as disagreements over the amount of independence given to children by parents or they can reflect issues of a moral or environmental nature, such as the treatment of young offenders or the building of roads on green-belt land. Children should be aware that

they are being asked to play a role which may or may not express their own point of view. It should be pointed out that they will be allowed to express their own points of view after the drama. It is important to speak in the manner of a radio presenter throughout the drama, in order to sustain the children's belief in the imaginary context.

Preparation

If using a cassette player with a built-in microphone, place this in a prominent position in the classroom. Make a sign saying 'On Air'. Prepare two sentences expressing opposing points of view on a topic or an issue. For example:
▲ We think violent videos and TV programmes are harmful and should be banned.
▲ We feel that present rules about violent videos and TV programmes are good enough and should not be changed.

Using a different coloured felt-tipped pen for each sentence, write each one on a large piece of white sugar paper and place both sheets on the wall, where everyone can see them.

Prepare some questions that will open up key aspects of the debate, such as: 'Does watching violent TV programmes make people more violent?' or 'Do parents who take their children to school make them too soft?'

Make one copy of photocopiable page 117 and write your questions in the appropriate place on the script outline. Make one copy per child of photocopiable page 118.

Resources needed

Photocopiable pages 117 and 118, a piece of A4 card folded to stand up on a table, two large pieces of white sugar paper, writing materials, a cassette player with a built-in microphone (optional).

What to do

Invite the children to take part in an imaginary radio show called 'People meet people' in which they will be given points of view and asked to take on roles as an invited audience of adults. Refer to the sentences on the two large sheets to explain the topic or issue. Discuss some possible arguments for each side and write these down on the sheets in note form, under the appropriate sentences.

Divide the class in half and allocate each half a point of view. Make sure that each half can see the relevant sheet with their arguments written on it. Pair each child with someone who has been given the same point of view. Ask the children to each fill in a copy of photocopiable page 118 to decide what sort of people they are and what they feel will be their best argument on the programme. Pairs can help each other and they can refer to their list on the wall.

Tell the children that you will take on the role of the radio presenter who is in charge of the show. Explain that, as the presenter, you will introduce and close the show using a script. You will also organize the proceedings and tell them when they can speak. Tell the children that when the sign saying 'On Air' is placed on your table, the drama will begin and the programme will start. (Tell them if you are using a real cassette.) Explain that when you take the sign off the table, the drama will stop.

Place the sign on the table and introduce the programme by reading from the script (photocopiable page 117). Refer to the script as a guide throughout the show to maintain the belief. Make sure you speak to the children as if they were adults and try to ensure that everyone has a chance to speak. Put in your own points of view if you need to move things on or extend a point made by a child.

Take down the sign to stop the drama. Find out how many children had to put forward a point of view they disagreed with and discuss this in terms of acting a part. Ask the children if anything they heard in the drama made them question or change their original point of view. After a brief discussion, ask the children to express their current views by pointing to the sentence they agree with most.

Suggestion(s) for extension

Ask more able children to predict what the opposition will select as their best argument (from the list on the wall) and tell them to prepare and/or write out a response. Encourage more confident children to give reasons for their opinions in role.

Suggestion(s) for support

Allow less confident children to work with those who are more confident when preparing their argument. Include questions suited to the less confident children among those sent in by the listeners and direct these questions accordingly. For example, should children be allowed to go to the supermarket on their own? Should younger children go to bed before older children? Why are the villagers complaining about the traffic going through the village? Why do lorries and buses cause more problems than cars or bikes going through the village?

Assessment opportunities

Note children's ability to develop and explain ideas, share opinions and adapt their vocabulary, tone, pace and style to the needs of the drama.

Opportunities for IT

The children could begin the activity by watching pre-recorded parts of a radio or TV chat show. If the school has access to a video camera, this could be used to record the children's own work and then replayed at the end of the session to stimulate discussion and evaluation of their work. Some children could operate the camera during the recording.

Display ideas

The children can draw a picture of themselves during the show. Ask them to include a large thought or speech bubble containing the point they felt most strongly about during the discussion. These can be displayed under the heading 'People meet people – what do *you* think!'

Reference to photocopiable sheets

Photocopiable page 117 is intended to be used as the radio presenter's script in the drama and can be used for a number of topics or issues. Photocopiable page 118 is provided to help each child decide on a role and an argument in preparation for the drama.

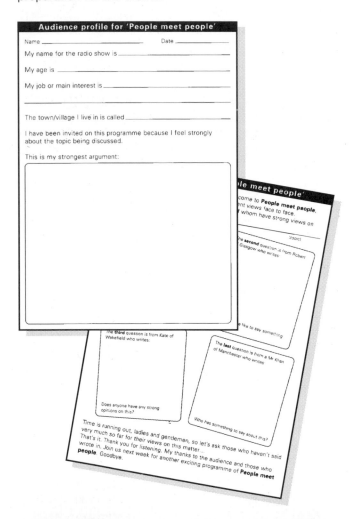

A CLASS STORY

To use role-play to devise and perform stories for a specified audience.

†† *Whole class and groups.*

🕑 *Session One: 60 minutes. Session Two: 30–45 minutes.*

Previous skills/knowledge needed

Children should be able to identify the beginning, middle and end of a simple story.

Key background information

This activity uses the imaginary role of a children's storyteller on the local radio as a stimulus for story-making. Throughout the drama you will need to collect the children's responses, as if you intend to pass them on to the storyteller. It is important to maintain this imaginary focus throughout the lessons. Session One can take place in the classroom but Session Two needs a large space. The sessions should be separated by no longer than a week.

Preparation

Session One: make one copy of photocopiable page 119. Write the words 'The Journey' as a heading on a large sheet of white sugar paper. Add the words 'Who? Why? Where?' Place the sheet out of sight in the classroom but prepare a place to put it, so that everyone will be able to see it and you will be able to write on it. Set up the cassette player and a blank tape in a corner of the room with four empty chairs around it. (You will need to use the children's ideas from Session One to produce a tape recording, which will be played at the beginning of Session Two.) Session Two: set up a cassette player to play your pre-recorded tape.

Resources needed

Photocopiable page 119, a large sheet of white sugar paper, writing materials, a cassette player with a built-in microphone and two blank tapes, a large space for Session Two.

DRAMA

What to do
Session One

Ask the class to imagine that they have received a letter from a well-known children's storyteller who works for the local radio station. Explain that on the word 'Action' you will talk to them as if they have really received the letter. Explain that you will stop the drama with the word 'Freeze'. Read out the letter on photocopiable page 119.

Fix the sheet of sugar paper to the wall and collect some ideas from the children for the 'Who? Why? Where?' questions, to start the story of a journey for the storyteller. Quickly decide on an answer to each question and write these on the paper using a felt-tipped pen. If there are any disagreements, stress that time is at a premium and that you will have to make the decisions.

Now organize the class into groups, with four children in each group, and ask each group to make up something that happens in the middle of the story. Explain that there will not be time to write down these ideas and so they will be recorded onto a cassette and sent to the radio storyteller.

Explain the following procedures to the class, before they start to work in groups:

▲ Each group should listen to everyone's ideas and then select one idea or put a few ideas together.

▲ Each group should select a storyteller(s) who is willing to record the group's idea onto the tape that will be sent to the radio storyteller. The group storyteller(s) should be given the chance to practise in front of his or her group. The group must act as directors. They must check that their storyteller(s) can communicate their idea clearly and accurately. Each storyteller must be given at least two opportunities to practise.

▲ Each group has about ten minutes to come up with an idea and five minutes to listen to their storyteller(s) and make suggestions.

Visit each group to support and advise. Ensure that all groups have an idea, however simple. Groups can share out the storytelling if they wish.

Invite each group to sit around the cassette player while their storyteller(s) records their idea, watched by the rest of the class. Remind the children that this tape will be sent to the radio storyteller, along with the sheet of paper outlining the start of the story.

An ending now has to be decided. Collect ideas and decide upon a suitable ending to write on the sheet. Use a different coloured felt-tipped pen from the one used for the start of the story. Promise to send the sheet and tape to the radio storyteller and promise to let the children listen to the storyteller's next broadcast, who will be using their ideas to tell his or her latest story, entitled 'The Journey'. Say the word 'Freeze' to stop the drama. Explain that they will hear the complete story at the start of the next drama lesson, when they will be asked to listen to it as if it were being broadcast on a local radio station.

After the lesson, organize the children's ideas into a story and tell the story onto the tape as if you are the radio storyteller. Start the tape with the words: *Hello children. Welcome to 'Storyslot', the programme that tells stories with children in mind. My name is Sam Harris and today we have a new story called 'The Journey', made up by some children at .... School. I hope you like it as much as I do.* Use the last words suggested by the children to conclude the story and then sign off with the words: *Thanks for listening and thanks to the children of .... class for such a wonderful story. Tune in next week, same time, for another 'Storyslot'. Goodbye.*

Session Two

Ask the children to imagine that they are listening to the storyteller telling their story on the radio, as they listen to your pre-recorded tape. Warn them that you have recorded it, so they will recognize your voice in role as the storyteller. Ask for the children's comments on the story in terms of its appeal to a radio audience.

Ask the children to imagine that the story was so popular that it was made into a story tape and sold in shops nationally. Then a TV company decided to make it into a new programme for television. The TV company asked the children if the story could be split up into sections, so that parts could be mimed by animated drawings and other parts could be narrated. Discuss this and suggest that they try to mime some of the events in the story, as you narrate.

Select parts of the story with a potential for mime. All the children should mime each section according to your narration, as if they were all playing one of the characters. Sometimes they may need to work in pairs as two characters. Discuss how each section could be mimed before starting the section.

DRAMA

Ask the class if they think their story would have commercial appeal as a realistic video and ask them to justify their opinions. Ask the children to work in groups to think of ideas for a poster, advertising the story on video.

Suggestion(s) for extension
Ask more confident groups to make a freeze-frame to illustrate their idea for the middle of the story (see 'Significant moments' on page 18).

Suggestion(s) for support
Help less confident children to decide on one simple idea for the middle of the story, and suggest that they record their idea pictorially. Offer to record this idea onto the tape on their behalf if necessary.

Assessment opportunities
Note the children's ability to work creatively in a group and their skills in selecting appropriate ideas for the middle of a story. Assess their levels of confidence in speaking onto a tape and their ability to express themselves in mime.

Opportunities for IT
Children could use a word processor to write the outline of the beginning of the story. They could also use an art or desktop publishing package to create a poster for their story or to create an exciting and stimulating inlay card for the audio cassette version.

Performance ideas
The story can be performed to a wider audience using a narrator, with freeze-frames or short sequences of mime.

Display ideas
Children can work in groups to produce a comic-strip version of the story for display.

Letter from Sam Harris, the radio storyteller

radio*live*

PO Box 343

Dear Children

Please can you help me? My name is Sam Harris. I tell children's stories on Radio Live at 5 o'clock every Wednesday. I usually have a writer to make up the stories for me, but my writer has been taken ill and cannot provide me with a story for this week. When I asked the director of the radio station if she could find me another writer, she said there wouldn't be enough time to contact anyone. She told me to write this week's story myself. I am useless at making up stories for children. I don't know what to do.

This week's story is advertised as being about two children aged seven to eleven years old who go on a journey. I am writing to ask for your help because you will know the kind of stories children like to hear. I must have an outline of the story within the next 24 hours to meet the deadline for recording the programme. Can you think of a story and send me the outline, on paper or on an audio cassette, as soon as possible? If I use your story I will tell the listeners that it was yours. Thanking you in anticipation.

Best wishes from

Sam Harris

Reference to photocopiable sheet
Photocopiable page 119 provides a letter to the children from the radio storyteller.

FAIRY TALES

To develop skills in devising and performing plays for a specific audience.

†† *Whole class and small groups.*

🕐 *Session One: 30–45 minutes. Session Two: 45–60 minutes.*

Previous skills/knowledge needed
Children should be familiar with the story of Cinderella.

Key background information
This activity needs a careful introduction to avoid a situation in which children see the subject matter as too infantile. It should be introduced as a way of performing to young children and as a way of learning a particular dramatic technique. The activity is spread over two sessions which should be separated by no more than a week.

Preparation
Make one copy of photocopiable pages 120 and 121. Make one copy of photocopiable page 122 for every three children. Use a bright coloured felt-tipped pen to write the names of the main characters of *Cinderella* on individual Post-It notes.

Resources needed
Photocopiable pages 120, 121 and 122, Post-It notes, flip chart or board, writing materials.

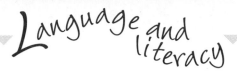

What to do
Session One

Explain that you are going to teach the children a particular technique for performing plays which relies on a narrator (storyteller) and mime. Tell the children that this technique is particularly useful when performing plays for young children. Explain that you would like to demonstrate the technique using a play intended for younger children. The play tells the story of Cinderella.

Explain that the first run-through will be like a silent movie, to get an idea of the play as a whole. Mention that this technique is sometimes used by actors before they learn their lines for a play. Performers will be asked to mime the actions at a fairly realistic pace, according to the words of the narrator. Stress that accuracy of mime is not required at this stage. The children should respond spontaneously to the narrative using mimed actions wherever they can to keep the story going.

Choose children to represent the main characters. Place the characters' names on their clothing using Post-It notes. Ask the rest of the class to play the parts of guests who are at the ball.

In consultation with the children, use a few chairs to make an outline set for the first scene in Cinderella's kitchen. Then plan the set for the ball and for a room in Cinderella's house. Ask some children to be stagehands so that chairs can be rearranged with a minimum of fuss, to create the sets as needed. Main characters should sit near the acting area to be ready to move onto the set.

Read the narrative (photocopiable pages 120 and 121) and let the characters respond in mime, where they can. This first run-through may be amusing or even confusing, as children experiment with the mime and try to work out their entrances and exits. Most errors should be overlooked on the first attempt, in the interests of keeping the action moving. Once the story has been completed, repeat the exercise at a slower pace, for a better quality run-through.

Session Two

Ask the children to help you to make up a modern version of *Cinderella* to suit older children. Suggest that it could be made more serious by focusing on problems in stepfamilies or more amusing by changing the names and the incidents. For example, the story could be about a boy called Cinderfella who wanted to go to Wembley to meet his football hero, or a girl called Cindy who won a ticket to see her favourite singer and wasn't allowed to go. Fairy godmothers can take different forms and the prince can be a hero of some kind. The wedding can just be a party if necessary. Discuss a few versions and write the ideas on the board.

Put the children into threes and give each group one copy of photocopiable page 122. Ask each group to make some brief notes on an outline for their modern version and then write a short narrative for any *one* of the scenes. After they have written their narration, they should try out the mimes, to see if they are workable. Make it clear that funny scenes should not be rude or silly.

Bring the class back together and let groups try out their modern scenes, using other members of the class to make up the cast if necessary. Groups should be given the option of reading their own narration and/or acting in their scene or letting others read and perform it on their behalf. After each scene, ask the class to identify anything that would appeal to an older audience.

Suggestion(s) for extension

Ask groups of more confident children to work in threes to write the narration for *The Three Little Pigs* or *The Three Billy Goats Gruff* and then work out the mimes. Each group will be able to act their play themselves, with one narrator and two actors. Children can play more than one part, using Post-It notes with their characters' names on different items of clothing.

Suggestion(s) for support

Choose simple parts for less confident children in Session One or ask them to be stagehands. During Session Two, let less confident groups concentrate on just one scene from a version on the board, and offer them your own support as they work out the scene. Encourage them to choose a simple scene that they can work on to achieve a good result.

Assessment opportunities

This activity tests children's listening skills and reveals their confidence in using mime. It also provides an opportunity to assess children's ability to subvert a familiar text.

Opportunities for IT

Some groups of children could use a word processor to write their scene from the modern version of the Cinderella story. They should be encouraged to write directly using the word processor and then draft and redraft their story to create a final copy.

If each group uses a word processor, the different scenes can be merged into a single document and the complete text published as a new version of *Cinderella*. Illustrations could be added to the story. These could be created using an art package, merging different clip-art pictures together or scanning children's own line drawings to create a digital image which can be used within the word-processed story.

Performance ideas

Any of the versions of *Cinderella* can be drafted/extended and rehearsed to produce a whole-class performance for a wider audience, perhaps during a Book Week or for a Christmas production. The original version of *Cinderella* would be suitable for performing to children in Years R/1 (P1/2), with a confident reader(s) as the narrator(s).

Reference to photocopiable sheets

Photocopiable pages 120 and 121 provide the narrative for the mimed version of *Cinderella*. Photocopiable page 122 provides children with a framework to help them to write a narration for their modern version of *Cinderella*.

THE UNFINISHED STORY

To build confidence in developing a story, using a range of drama strategies.

✝✝ *Whole class and groups.*

🕐 *Session One: 30–45 minutes. Session Two: 30–45 minutes.*

Previous skills/knowledge needed

This activity works best when children have had some previous experience in working in whole-group drama.

Key background information

The open-ended nature of this activity requires the teacher to draw upon a variety of drama strategies without any detailed pre-planning. It also requires some confidence in working as teacher-in-role. The activity is spread over two sessions which should be separated by no longer than a week.

Preparation

Make four name cards, one for each of the following occupations: builders / food gatherers / potters / cloth makers. Arrange four chairs around three sides of the room and place a name card on each chair. Drape some cloth over a piano stool or a small table so that the cloth reaches the floor. Place this at the side of the hall where there are no chairs. Place another chair beside the stool. Make a copy of the story on photocopiable page 123, roll it into a scroll shape and tie it with a ribbon. Place this out of sight, under the stool. Make a cloak or scarf out of a piece of rough material such as hessian or wool, to wear as teacher-in-role. Place this on the chair next to the stool.

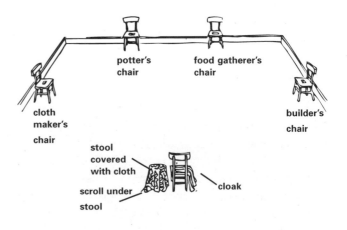

Resources needed

A large space, five chairs, a stool or small table, a plain rich-coloured cloth (to cover the stool), four pieces of card, writing materials, photocopiable page 123, a piece of ribbon, hessian or woollen cloth (big enough to use as a scarf or cloak), a whistle.

What to do

Session One

Tell the children that you would like them to help you to make up and act out a story. Explain that you already know the start of the story, but you do not know the middle of the story or the end. Explain that you will use drama to take them through the start of the story and then you will stop to collect their ideas for the rest of the story.

The story is about a group of villagers who lived on a remote island. Many years ago, something happened on the island that made one part of the village decide to cut itself off from the world and become self-sufficient. No one knows what this event was, but the people who cut themselves off built a high wall around their houses. For the last 50 years, no one has been seen going in or out of the village behind the wall.

Explain that you would like the children to play the parts of the people who lived behind the wall. Ask the children to imagine that the room represents the village and that the chairs represent where people live. Explain that in this community, the area you live in depends upon the kind of work you do and there are four main occupations. Allocate the jobs of builders, food gatherers, potters and cloth makers to the groups. Briefly discuss what these jobs would entail in a self-sufficient community and ask each person to think of two tasks that they usually perform on an ordinary day in relation to their job. Make some suggestions, such as builders visiting houses to ask if anything needs repairing and then building some wooden furniture. Let children talk in pairs to make these decisions. Make it clear that these jobs will be carried out in mime, but they must talk to each other as if they were really the people in the community.

Tell the children that, when you wear the scarf, you will play the part of the Elder of the community, who gives advice and lets people use his herb garden to make medicines. Explain that the Elder usually stays near his house so that anyone can ask for help at any time, and that he is the only person in the community who can remember anything about what life was like before the wall was built. However, the Elder will not speak about this time. No one is allowed to go near the wall, which is now overgrown with moss and plants. The Elder lives near the area of the stool, which is part of the Elder's house.

Ask each child to decide which job they will do first in the drama. Explain that when you say the word 'Action', the community will come to life, and when you blow a whistle and say the word 'Freeze', they must stop. Explain that you will start with a freeze-frame of a moment at the beginning of a typical day, when everyone is ready to start work. Ask all the children to stand in a 'frozen' position in their area of the community and start the drama on the word 'Action'.

During the drama, try to wait for children to come to you as the Elder. Give advice on their problems and recommend various herbs from your garden for any health problems. Use a formal language register for this role, as a kindly but authoritative figure. Stop the drama after several minutes and take off the scarf to come out of role as the Elder.

Call the children together in front of the stool. Explain that at the end of every day, the community would gather in front of the Elder's house. Every night the Elder reminded them of how lucky they were to live in safety behind the wall. Every night he told them a story with a message. The Elder never wrote down the stories.

Tell the children that one night the Elder produced a story written on a scroll, tied with a ribbon. Take out the scroll from under the stool and explain that you will start the drama again at the moment when the Elder revealed the scroll. Start the drama again on the word 'Action'.

In role as the Elder, explain that you have been waiting for this night for a long time. Now it has come, you are afraid because after tonight, nothing will be the same again. Explain that you have kept this story hidden for many years and you will now read the story from the scroll. Tell them that this story is a special story because every word written down is true. Do not allow the children to ask any questions at this point. If any should arise, tell the children that all will be answered in time. Keep this moment as serious as possible and read the scroll with reverence.

After the reading, keep in role as the Elder and tell the children that whatever happens tonight, you will always care about them and that whatever they do, they must keep together. Stop the drama immediately, saying the word 'Freeze' quietly as you take off the scarf to come out of role. Tell the children that you will now tell them what happened in the next 24 hours. Use the following script as a guide:

After the story, the Elder would speak no more and went into his house, leaving the people very confused. The next day, when the people started their work, they noticed that the Elder was missing and so was the scroll. (Place the scroll to one side and ask the children to imagine that it has gone.) *When they finally looked around they noticed that a door had appeared in the wall. It was obvious from the moss that the door had recently been opened. The people decided to hold a meeting to decide what to do.*

Explain that you would like to restart the drama where the people are at the meeting. Ask the children if you can now play the part of the Elder's best friend, who has called the meeting. In this part you will act as chairperson for the meeting. Sit the children in a circle or in two semicircles and restart the drama. Let as many children speak as

possible at the meeting and try to elicit suggestions as to why the Elder has gone and what should be done. Remind the community of the Elder's request for them to keep together. After a few ideas have been suggested about what to do, try to come to an agreement on the first thing that must be done. Then stop the drama and explain that this is the end of the first part of the story.

Tell the children that in the next drama lesson they will be asked to think about how the story could be developed. Collect some initial possibilities before concluding the lesson. For example:

▲ They meet someone who can tell them where the Elder has gone.

▲ They find the Elder but cannot reach him, and need to solve some problems or do certain tasks before reaching the Elder.

▲ They meet the Elder, who needs their help to solve a problem.

Session Two

Ask the children to recap on the story so far, and explain that you will need them to suggest ideas on how the story should develop in the drama. Make it clear that you will be selecting ideas based on whether or not they can easily be acted out rather than whether they are good ideas for a story. You may suggest that the children write down any unused ideas after the drama, to provide material for future drama lessons.

Focus on collecting ideas for the next main event in the story and discuss ways in which it can be acted out by the whole group.

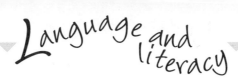

Act out the story, one main event at a time. Avoid acting out unnecessary details, and maintain the focus on the particular event. You can take on other roles yourself and/ or ask children to take on roles temporarily, to move the story on. After each event, discuss what the children would like to happen next; choose one of their ideas and then discuss how to act it out before putting it into practice. Keep the events short and make sure the acting out is achievable. One or two cloaks can be used to identify new roles, but try to keep props and costumes to a minimum.

About 15 minutes before the end of the lesson, encourage the children to think about an appropriate ending to the story, so that other events can work towards it. Then before performing the final event, talk about how this could be made special or more theatrical by using music, chants or symbolic actions.

After the last part of the story, ask the children to identify what they felt worked best in the drama and which parts they would want to change or improve.

Suggestion(s) for extension
After some initial ideas from the whole class at the start of Session Two, ask more confident children to demonstrate how the next event in the story might be acted out. Use this as a basis for making a final decision about how the next event will be acted out by the class. Let more confident children play other roles in these events, if the opportunity arises.

Suggestion(s) for support
If the whole class find acting out stories difficult, ask them to act out just one event and an ending in Session Two. Support less confident children in Session One by pairing them with more confident children. Give less confident children parts suited to their levels of confidence when acting out the events in Session Two.

Assessment opportunities
Note children's ability to pose pertinent questions, explore, develop and explain ideas and plan a sequence of events. Look for children who are confident in acting out the prearranged sequences in Session Two.

Performance ideas
With rehearsal, parts of the story can be acted out by small groups and performed to a wider audience, using a narrator as a link.

Display ideas
The whole story, or parts of the story, can be written onto an opened scroll and displayed alongside the other scroll as part of the history of the imaginary community.

Reference to photocopiable sheet
Photocopiable page 123 contains the story read by the Elder and can be used as the scroll for the drama.

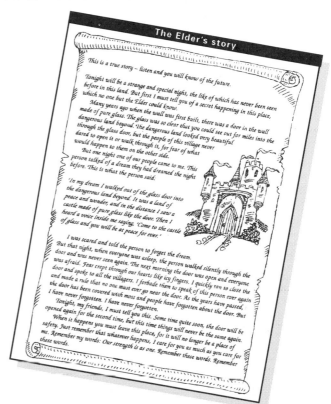

THE PATHWAY

To use physical theatre and spoken thoughts to create a character and stimulate improvisation.

Whole class and small groups.

45–60 minutes.

Previous skills/knowledge needed
This activity works best when the children have had some experience in using freeze-frames, spoken thoughts and small group improvisations.

Key background information
This activity uses teacher-in-role and physical theatre as a focus for the development of the drama. It provides a starting point for drama but can also be used as a stimulus for creative writing.

Preparation

Select a scarf or jacket, and bag or holdall, to represent the kind of character you will take on the role of in the drama. Fix a sheet of sugar paper to the wall, and attach a felt-tipped pen to the wall at the side of the paper.

Resources needed

A large space, a scarf or jacket and a bag or holdall for the character in the drama, a large sheet of sugar paper, writing materials.

What to do

Explain that the following activity will help the children to build up a story about a character for drama. Tell the children that the character in the drama regularly walks along a particular route. The route is not an easy one and takes the person over, under and around things on the way. Explain that when you put on the clothing and pick up the bag, you will take on the role of this person walking the route. Ask the class to work in pairs or threes to make your route with their bodies. Explain that they must make sure you will be able to walk over, under or around the shapes they make. Tell them that they can make arched shapes for you to walk under or they can join hands low down on the floor for you to walk over. They can make twists and turns to make it interesting, but make it clear that the character must be able to walk along the route without problems.

When the route is ready, have a trial run and walk along it to see if you can negotiate it. Make any necessary adaptations and then tell the class to come out of their positions, but stay along the route while you discuss the next task. Ask each child to be your eyes as you walk the route. Explain that as you pass by each pair or three, you will pause for a moment and this will be their cue to tell everyone what the character can see at this point. Children should repeat the same words in chorus, for example, if a pair have made a bridge, they will both say 'a bridge' when you stop near them. Now let the children make the pathway, and walk through slowly, pausing by each pair in turn to let them say what you see. If a pair should forget what to say, just move on without comment. Walk down the path as if you are worried or unhappy about something. (This creates a tension which will develop into the focus of the drama and move it forward.)

Collect the children together and summarize what the pathway looks like to the character. Now ask them to imagine that there are houses overlooking the pathway. Ask the children to stand with their partners along the line of the pathway as if they are watching from the houses near the pathway. Explain that this time you would like them to be the people watching the character walk along the route. This time as you walk past and pause by them, each pair must speak out what they think about the character. They can say two separate thoughts, repeat the same thought or say one thought in chorus. Talk about what they might assume about the character from what they have observed so far. Make it clear that the people in the houses may or may not know much about this character but they will have an opinion about this person because they have watched him or her walk the path every day for a long time. Give the children a few minutes to make up their spoken thoughts. Then walk along the line of the previous pathway and pause by each pair to listen to their spoken thoughts. Move on if any child forgets what to say.

Now collect everything that has been said about the character and write these comments in summary on the sugar paper on the wall. Suggest that the children give the character a suitable name. Avoid amusing names, unless you intend the character to be amusing. Talk about why this person has reached this point in his or her life and what could have happened in the past. Decide on some possibilities and write these on the sheet on the wall.

Choose or invent a situation from the character's past involving a large group, such as a wedding, christening or other celebration attended by several people. Other situations might include a market, café or airport lounge. The scene will include all the class in a whole-group improvisation. The scene can be brought to life before the character enters and then stopped after the character has interacted with some of the people. Keep this short and be prepared to stop the improvisation and bring just one group to life to see how they are interacting with the main character. After the improvisation, discuss what happened and how it might have affected the character's life.

Put pairs or a pair and a three together to make four or five in each group and ask each group to prepare a freeze-frame showing something else of importance that happened in this character's life. Then let each group perform their freeze-frames. They must also be prepared to explain their ideas.

Conclude the lesson by discussing what might happen to the character in the future. This could form the basis for further drama work or written work.

Suggestion(s) for extension

More confident groups can be allowed to produce short improvisations instead of the freeze-frames. However, they should be encouraged to start and finish their improvisations with appropriate freeze-frames, and perhaps choose a significant moment within their scene to freeze and speak aloud the character's thoughts.

Suggestion(s) for support

Put less confident children in a group of three to make the pathway and encourage them to choose a physical position that they will be able to maintain without falling over. Help less confident groups choose a simple moment to depict as a freeze-frame of the character's past.

Assessment opportunities

Assess children's skills in physical theatre and in improvising drama in a large group. Look also for children who can initiate ideas, listen to and adapt the ideas of others and follow ideas through to a conclusion during the discussions.

Opportunities for IT

The children could create an electronic photograph album of the various freeze-frames using a multimedia authoring package. Each freeze-frame could be photographed using a digital camera, or scanned from a conventional photograph. The digital images could then be used within the authoring package to create a series of linked pages which highlight the different parts of the story or characters within it.

The presentation could start with a title page which lists the different scenes, so that by selecting a particular scene the user is taken to that scene. Alternatively, the scenes could be linked so that the full set of scenes can be replayed from start to finish automatically. Pages could also be set up so that the user can 'browse' from scene to scene.

The children's own voices can be recorded using a microphone attached to the computer. These sound-clips can be linked to the thought bubbles, so that when the user clicks on the bubble the speech is heard. If several freeze-frames are worked on, these could be put together in the same presentation to create a series of freeze-frames.

If the school has a video camera and access to a digitizer, you could include video-clips of the scenes, moving from the freeze-frame at the start to the video action, and back to the freeze-frame. Recorded video-clips take up a large amount of memory, so you will need access to a large hard drive, network or other storage medium to undertake this work.

Performance ideas

The freeze-frames can be performed as photographs in the character's photo album. The character looks at the album and when he or she begins to daydream, the freeze-frames come to life as flashbacks.

Display ideas

The words recorded on the sugar paper can be written inside an outline figure of the character. This can be a central focus for drawings depicting key moments of the character's life, as revealed in the freeze-frames or the scenes. Each drawing can be given a title, as in a photograph album or alternatively, thought bubbles can be added to focus on the feelings of the moment.

It's now or never!

REMEMBER, REMEMBER

To use role-play and whole-group drama to create an opportunity for recall and reflection on a story.

†† *Pairs and whole class.*

🕐 *Session One: 15–20 minutes. Session Two: 20–30 minutes.*

Previous skills/knowledge needed

Children should have read the chosen story and be familiar with the sequence of events.

Key background information

This activity is divided into two sessions. The role-play exercise in Session One is intended to be used as an introductory activity to Session Two and so the gap between the two sessions should not be too long. Session One can be carried out in the classroom but Session Two needs a large space. Session Two requires the children to recall and reflect upon some of the larger events in the chosen story from the perspective of eyewitnesses, such as the farmers in *The Iron Man* by Ted Hughes (Faber & Faber) or the Oompa-Loompas in *Charlie and the Chocolate Factory* by Roald Dahl (Puffin).

Preparation

Make one copy per group of photocopiable pages 124 and 125 and two copies per group of photocopiable page 126.

Resources needed

A copy of the chosen story (see 'Key background information'), photocopiable pages 124, 125 and 126, writing materials, an outdoor jacket, notebook, a large space for Session Two.

What to do
Session One

Organize the class into pairs and put the pairs into groups of four. Name each pair in a group either A or B. Ask the children to sit in pairs within their groups. Give out copies of photocopiable page 124 to the pairs named A and copies of photocopiable page 125 to the other pairs named B. Read through the sheets with the class and explain the task carefully. Explain that pairs of eyewitnesses to a crime are to be interviewed by pairs of newspaper journalists. The first sheet shows a picture of an imaginary 'smash and grab' raid taken by hidden cameras. Pair B should take on the role of journalists, who interview pair A as eyewitnesses to the crime depicted on the sheet. The journalists should use the questions on photocopiable page 126 to help them interview their witnesses, writing answers to the questions in note form on the photocopiable sheet. Give pairs some time to prepare before the interviews.

As groups finish, let the pairs swap roles so that pair B become the witnesses and pair A become the journalists. Give pair B a copy of photocopiable page 125 to use as the picture of their crime and give the journalists their own copy of photocopiable page 126.

Use a narrative style to tell the children that after work was completed, someone came into the garden asking to speak to them. Explain that the person was wearing a jacket and carrying a notebook and pen. Tell the children that you will pretend to be this person when you put on the jacket. In role as this person, explain that you are a newspaper reporter from the Daily Gazette. You are writing an article on the events that are commemorated in the garden and wish to ask the witnesses some questions. Ask questions that require the children to recall the sequence of events and reveal their feelings as witnesses. Ask them to speculate about what the main characters might have felt like and why they took the actions they did. Pretend to write the answers in shorthand in your notebook. (Be careful to ask the questions as if you are a journalist, not as a teacher who already knows the answers.) Be prepared to invent details such as your name, the address of your paper and when you think the article will be published. Then stop the drama and take off the jacket to come out of role.

Session Two

Tell the children that the drama is about something that might have happened to a group of people who witnessed some of the events in the story they have been reading. Specify exactly who the eyewitnesses will be in relation to the chosen story, for instance the farmers in *The Iron Man* or the Oompa-Loompas in *Charlie and the Chocolate Factory*. Explain that the drama takes place some time after the end of the story and will not be a re-enactment of the story in the book. Ask the children to play the parts of the witnesses. They should imagine that the room is a derelict garden belonging to one of the witnesses. Define the areas of the room to be used in the drama.

Ask the children to arrange themselves in a large circle, as if they were standing around the edge of the garden. Tell the children that the drama begins at the moment when one of the witnesses, played by yourself, calls the others to a meeting in the garden. Explain that, while the children will be allowed to talk to each other when in role, they will need to mime any actions. Use the words 'Action' and 'Freeze' to start and stop the drama each time.

Start the drama and take on the role of one of the witnesses. Ask the children for some help to make the area into some kind of commemorative garden, so that the events you all witnessed will never be forgotten. Ask for suggestions on what would be appropriate and why. Try to talk as if you are genuinely seeking ideas, rather than speaking as a teacher collecting answers. Join the children as they mime making the garden. After a few minutes, or when the children appear to have finished, stop the drama and come out of role. Tell the children to sit down as if in the newly completed garden area.

Explain that after the garden was completed, a number of newspaper journalists arrived at the garden. They asked the eyewitnesses some detailed questions about the garden and about the events they had witnessed. Using the groups in Session One, ask one pair to take on the roles of journalists. They must interview the other pair, who will be in role as witnesses. Before starting the drama again, discuss what the journalists might ask. Separate the pairs in each group and give them a few minutes to prepare before restarting the drama with the interviewing in the garden. Groups who finish before the others can exchange roles and conduct another interview.

Suggestion(s) for extension

Ask more confident groups to perform their interviews to the class in Sessions One and Two. After the drama, ask confident groups to make their bodies into a statue to commemorate the main events in the story and let them show these to the class.

Suggestions for support

In the role-play exercise, let less confident children work in a group with those who will include them, and be prepared to support them by temporarily taking on a role within their group. Work alongside any children who need support in making the garden. When in role as the journalist, you can differentiate by directing appropriate questions to the less confident children.

Assessment opportunities

Assess children's ability to respond appropriately in role and assess their corporate knowledge of the story. Look for children who perform confidently in the paired role-plays.

Display ideas

Children can be asked to draw pictures of what they think the garden looked like. These can be displayed around a commemorative verse made up by the children about the event.

References to photocopiable sheets

Photocopiable pages 124 and 125 depict the crimes for the witnesses in the role-play exercise and photocopiable page 126 provides the questions for the journalists.

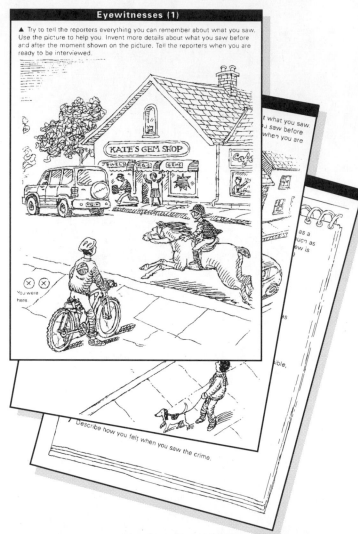

IN MY SHOES

To develop confidence in using hot-seating to explore perspectives on literary texts.

†† *Whole class and pairs.*

🕐 *Session One: 20 minutes. Session Two: 30 minutes.*

Previous skills/knowledge needed

Children need to know the sequence of events and the names of the central characters in the chosen story or poem. Some previous experience of hot-seating would be an advantage but is not essential.

Key background information

These activities are adaptations of the hot-seating strategy, in which a teacher or a child sits on a chair to answer questions, posed by the class, as if he or she were a character from the text. The length of time spent on each

session will depend upon the concentration levels of the class and their previous experience of hot-seating. The activities can be spread over two sessions or can be carried out in the same session. The second activity is designed to be used with class readers or where every child has access to the same text. The written preparation for the task in the second activity could be completed by individual children for homework.

Preparation
Clear a space at the front of the classroom. Place four empty chairs in a line in the space, facing the class.

Resources needed
Four chairs, rough paper, writing materials, copies of your chosen text (see 'Preparation'). Flip chart or board for support activity.

What to do
Session One
Choose four children to represent one of the main characters in your chosen text and ask them to sit on the chairs at the front of the classroom. Explain that these

children will be the voice of the character. When any one of them speaks, that will be the voice of the character. Make it clear that they will need to take turns at speaking and that you will tell them when you want them to speak. If one voice cannot answer, then you will ask the next voice.

Explain that this is a chance for the class to find out why the character might have behaved in a particular way and how the character might feel about the events in the text.

Discuss the best kinds of questions to ask the character. Distinguish between questions which ask for useful information, such as 'How did you feel when...?' and those which do not, such as 'What did you eat for your lunch?'

Organize the children into pairs and give them a few minutes to write down three or four questions to ask the character. They must not let the children in the hot-seat hear the questions. Tell the group in the hot-seat to predict what the class might ask them and then make up some answers. They should not let the class hear what they are saying. Stop the class when most pairs have at least one question.

Emphasize that listening to the answers is more important than being able to ask a question. Prepare them for the likelihood that other children will ask a question that is the same as one that they have included – tell them that if this happens, it means that it was probably a good question!

Ask the children to raise their hands if they have a question for the character. Start at one end of the line of four voices and ask the first child if he or she would like to answer. Allow other voices to elaborate on the original comment if appropriate. Move along the line of voices in turn, giving each voice the chance to be the first to answer a new question. Intervene to extend the questions and answers if necessary.

Session Two

Choose a pair of confident children to represent a main character from the text (or play this part yourself if necessary). Sit these children on chairs at the front of the classroom. Share out the other characters from the text among the other pairs of children, so that each pair is given one character between them. Include minor characters. Some pairs will be given the same character as other pairs, unless there are several characters in the text.

Explain that they will be asked to speak as if they were their character and will be asked to tell the main character what they feel about them. They are to use what they know of the text and make good guesses where little information is available. They should look at the text in their pairs and write down notes to help them to remember what to say. The children playing the main character must think about how they feel about the other characters in the text, but make it clear that they will be given help from yourself and the rest of the class if they need it. Before starting the task, collect one idea for each character from the whole group. Check that at least one pair representing each character has something to say before stopping the work.

Now go through each character in turn, asking each pair of children to say what they feel about the main character. Ask the class to comment and then ask the pair representing the main character to respond with their feelings. If any pair cannot think of a comment, ask the class to make suggestions on their behalf.

Suggestion(s) for extension

Extend the activity in Session Two by choosing two or three confident children to represent different minor characters from the text and ask them to improvise a conversation in which they talk to each other about how they feel about one of the main characters. Let them perform this to the class and then invite the class to comment on the feasibility of the opinions expressed in the improvisation. Ask each character in the improvisation to justify some of their opinions to the class, either in or out of role.

Suggestion(s) for support

In Session One, support less confident pairs by collecting ideas for appropriate questions from the class and writing these on the board for anyone to use if they wish. If the class is cautious in asking questions, ask questions yourself to maintain the activity. In Session Two, place less confident children with a more confident pair, to make a group of three.

Assessment opportunities

Assess children's confidence in speaking and listening in role. Look for children who are able to question and respond appropriately within an imaginary context. Note any children who are able to pose perceptive questions and those who are able to see a text from the perspective of a character.

Opportunities for IT

Children could record and present the responses from the hot-seating activity in the form of a diary using a word processor. Let them experiment with the text font and size so that the diary can be used as part of a display, and remind them to try to make sure that the text can be read from a distance.

Performance ideas

Ask some children to devise and perform an imaginary conversation between two of the characters who meet by accident in a new situation, for example in a café, in a shop or while walking in a garden.

Display ideas

Responses from the characters can be summarized, recorded and displayed in the form of diary entries.

Theatre skills

This chapter relates to drama as theatre and concentrates on drama as an art form in its own right. The activities will help the more cautious children to perform a piece of drama at a simple level, without anxiety. They will also encourage confident children to focus their contributions in a more structured and thoughtful way. Some children are able to produce improvisations of great length but these are often of poor quality. The activities in this chapter are intended to encourage children to strive for quality rather than quantity when performing.

This chapter also includes suggestions for script writing and for rehearsing and performing scripted plays. Children need plenty of opportunities to read plays in order to understand how scripts are organized and set out. An opportunity to see live theatre is also a great help, and visits to the theatre can be used to increase children's critical appreciation.

Improving children's confidence in theatre skills can raise their self-esteem, provide a means of artistic expression and help them become more critical of what they watch as an audience. This chapter provides children with an introduction to such skills and assumes little or no prior dramatic training or experience on the part of the children or the teacher. The activities are designed to encourage children to develop their theatre skills both as performers and as an audience.

DRAMA

SCRIPT ON TAPE

To develop skills in the writing and performance of scripted drama.

†† *Whole class and small groups.*

🕐 *About two hours (at least 40–50 minutes per session).*

Previous skills/knowledge needed

Children should be familiar with how simple playscripts are organized. They should be familiar with the characteristics of the work of the painter whose work is to be the focus for the script, for example LS Lowry or Van Gogh.

Key background information

The setting for this activity is an art gallery, and the subjects of the scripts are the paintings. However, the processes for script writing used in these sessions can also be applicable to other contexts and subject areas. Children usually enjoy reading their own scripts; a personal engagement and familiarity with their own scripts means that they are more likely to read them with meaning and expression. However, as children often find writing scripts difficult, and may need a considerable amount of support, they will be more amenable to drafting a small amount of text than to writing a script covering several pages. It is best to break up the script writing process into a number of stages, to ensure attention is paid to all aspects of writing and performing. The procedures used in this activity are tightly structured, and will enable most children to succeed. The sessions are designed to feed into each other, so the gap between each session should not be too long.

The audience for the script writing in these sessions comes from within a dramatic framework in which the end-product is the making of a security audio cassette for an art gallery. This helps to motivate the children, along with the knowledge that they will be required to read their scripts onto a tape in role as visitors to the art gallery. Reading scripts onto a tape also takes away the need to learn the lines and yet retains the need to read the material with expression. The children are asked to record their work in the presence of the rest of the class. This encourages them to take the script readings seriously and adds status to the work. If this is not practical, then arrange for groups to record their work in private, at convenient times during the school day. If you do this, make sure that you listen to each recording, before playing the tape to the rest of the class.

Preparation

Clear a space on a wall for two or three large prints of paintings by your chosen artist. Ensure that all the children will be able to see the prints when they are writing their scripts.

Prepare a cassette player to record the children reading their scripts. Make a large sign saying 'Silence please. Recording in progress'. Fold this sign so that it will stand on a table. Make simple signs for the art gallery – these should show the name of the painter and the names of the prints on display.

Prepare an area of the room where the children can sit to record their voices onto the audio cassette, a group at a time. This area should be visible to the rest of the class. Make one copy per child of photocopiable page 127.

Resources needed

Two or three large prints which characterize the work of your chosen painter, three or four pieces of card, photocopiable page 127, flip chart or board, lined paper, timers, writing materials, a cassette player with a built-in microphone and a blank tape.

What to do
Session One

Organize the children into groups of three (use pairs if the numbers don't work out for threes). Display the prints in a prominent position in the classroom, along with the information signs. Ask the children to imagine that the prints are paintings in an art gallery. Talk about what people might say about the paintings, both positive and negative, and write these in note form on the board. Now ask the children to imagine that, following an attempted burglary, the art gallery installed a security tape in every room to record voices and sounds that might be suspicious. This tape also picked up the voices of the visitors as they looked at the paintings. Explain that, when the art gallery listened to the tape, they discovered that most people looked at the paintings in groups of two or three and stayed talking for between half a minute to a minute, before moving on to the next set of paintings.

Invite the children to work in groups to make the imaginary security tape. Explain that they will need to invent the conversations, write them as scripts and record them onto a tape. Give each child one copy of photocopiable page 127. Explain that each scripted conversation must last between half a minute and a minute and should include good and bad comments about the paintings. They can use the notes on the board to help them. Make it clear that the script should sound realistic, as if it were really a tape-recording of visitors passing by and making comments.

Ask the groups to start by deciding on three (or two) characters for their script. Make it clear that these should be people who are visiting the art gallery. Once they have decided on the characters, they should decide who will play them. Each child should fill in a photocopiable sheet for their character, but encourage groups to work together.

When the sheets have been completed, give the groups some lined paper and make sure that they know how to set out a script, so that it is clear when each person is supposed to be speaking. Tell them to concentrate first on putting in the positive and negative comments spoken by the characters about the paintings. They should use their completed character sheets as a guide, and produce a rough draft. Groups need only write one copy, but make sure that they take turns at being the scribe. While the children are drafting their scripts, concentrate on ensuring that each group has a balance of positive and negative comments about the paintings.

When groups appear to be well on the way with the first draft, stop the work and ask the children to think about how to make their conversations sound realistic and interesting. Discuss some possibilities, such as arguments about the paintings, amusing comments, quarrelling children or even conversations about thefts and fakes. Suggest that the children focus on making the first and last lines sound as if the people are arriving and leaving the room. Discuss some possibilities before asking the children to resume their work.

As groups finish their drafting, tell them to quietly read their scripts aloud to time them. If the script lasts more or less than the allotted half to one minute, they should adjust

their work accordingly. Groups can time each other if appropriate. Groups who work slowly may not have time to do this. Such groups should estimate the length of their script reading by comparing their work to others' finished scripts. Collect in the drafts and mark them with a few suggestions for improvements.

Session Two

Once the draft copies have been amended, each child in the group should write or have a photocopy of their script to read out onto the tape. When everyone has their own copy of their script, tell the groups to practise their readings. Then stop them for a moment and explain that, because their scripts are being recorded on tape, they will be unable to use facial expressions or body movements to make them more interesting and so they must rely on reading with expression.

Write some feelings on the board. Choose those which might be appropriate for the context of the script, such as bored, pleased, curious, impatient, angry, surprised, tired. Take a line from one of the scripts and read it in a number of different ways to indicate some of the feelings on the board. Now repeat this with another line and ask the class to guess how you are feeling each time. Talk about how feelings can affect how people talk. Invite individual children to read a line as if they were feeling a particular way and ask the class to guess how the reader is feeling. If some children wish to talk with accents, make sure they will be portrayed sensitively and check that they will not cause offence to anyone before allowing it. Emphasize that accents are optional and should only be used if they can be maintained throughout the script reading.

Now tell the children to go back to their scripts and try to identify one or two places where the people would have a particular feeling. They should write a description to show how the person is feeling (in the margin, next to the appropriate lines) and then practise how the lines would be spoken to reveal that feeling. Some children may find

this difficult and will need you to help them to identify the feelings within their work. Choose easily identifiable feelings, for example you might suggest that the people would be feeling curious as they arrive to see the paintings and then feel pleased or bored as they talk about them.

Session Three

Set up the cassette player in an appropriate area of the classroom so that everyone can see it. Arrange three chairs around the cassette player so that the chairs do not directly face the class. Put the sign saying 'Silence please. Recording in progress' face down near the cassette player.

Give groups a few minutes to practise reading their scripts and then pair them up so that each group has an opportunity to read their script to another group. Ask those listening to check for clarity and understanding and to pick out the thing they liked best about the work.

When groups have finished reading to each other, explain that each group will be asked to come into the recording area to record themselves reading their scripts. Before this happens, let the class have a final rehearsal, all together. Organize this by asking all the groups to start their final rehearsal simultaneously, when you say the word 'Action'. Make it clear that, when groups finish their reading, they should fold their arms and wait in silence, until the last group has finished. Explain that you will time this rehearsal and if any group goes much over one minute you will tell them to stop.

bored
pleased
curious
impatient
angry

Collect in the scripts, so that children are not tempted to work on them while others are recording. Show the class the 'Silence' sign and ask them to treat the classroom like a recording studio. Explain that when the sign is on the table, everyone must be silent until you stop the tape and say the word 'Cut'.

Call out the groups in turn, to sit on the chairs and read their scripts onto the tape. If children falter, press the pause button as soon as possible to avoid the need to re-record. When all the groups have recorded their scripts, ask the class to listen to the whole cassette as if it were a security tape. Ask them to think about which parts they would pick out as being particularly good, while they are listening to the tape. Point out that negative comments about individuals will not be allowed. Ask them to judge the tape on whether it sounds realistic and interesting. Conclude the session by asking the children to give their own personal opinions about the paintings.

Suggestion(s) for extension
Ask more confident children to think about a security camera version of their script. Ask them to include a sketch showing what the people in their script might have looked like and what the room in the art gallery might have looked like when viewed on a security camera. Tell them to make a freeze-frame, showing a still picture of their characters on the security camera and let them perform this to the class.

Suggestion(s) for support
Encourage less confident children to invent lines that they can read and/or say easily. Encourage them to use simple phrases such as 'Look at these paintings over here'. If necessary suggest one or two suitable lines yourself and concentrate on making sure each child can remember when to say them. Less confident children may find it easier to remember when to speak if they are given the first lines of the conversation.

Assessment opportunities
Look for script writing that is organized, appropriate and interesting. Note where conversations follow a logical pattern and include variety and tension. Look for children who contribute ideas and develop the ideas of others in the group situation. Note any children who find it difficult to read with expression and any who lack confidence in reading aloud.

Opportunities for IT
Invite groups to use a word processor to make printed copies of their script. The final set of scripts can be collated and published as a class book of plays (see 'Display ideas'). Let some children use an art package to design a cover for the book.

More modern educational word processors, or presentation software, allow speech files to be linked to pages, which would make it possible to play back a recording of the performed script as the page is displayed.

Performance ideas
Let some groups choose their own or another group's script to perform as a representation of what was seen and heard on the art gallery's video camera.

Display ideas

Put the final scripts into a book of plays entitled 'Conversations in an art gallery'. Display this, along with the prints and any sketches the children might have made to represent their characters on a security camera (see 'Suggestion(s) for extension').

Reference to photocopiable sheet

Photocopiable page 127 is used as a simple writing frame to help children invent contrasting opinions for the characters. The completed sheets can be referred to during the subsequent script writing.

CAN YOU MIME IT?

To build confidence in the use of mime in performance.

†† *Whole class and pairs.*

⏱ *30–40 minutes.*

Previous skills/knowledge needed

Children should be able to read simple instructions.

Key background information

The purpose of this activity is to build children's confidence in using mime and to give them an opportunity to explore some possibilities. The main focus is on enjoyment and exploration but accurate and imaginative interpretations should also be encouraged.

Preparation

Make one copy of photocopiable page 128 and one copy of photocopiable page 129 and glue them onto separate pieces of thin A4 card. Cover each card with clear self-adhesive plastic film and then cut out the individual sections to make 12 small cards.

Resources needed

A large space, photocopiable pages 128 and 129, clear self-adhesive plastic film, scissors, adhesive.

What to do

Organize the class into pairs and ask everyone to stand with you in a circle. Tell the children to imagine that you have a ball in your hand. Throw and catch an imaginary ball as if it were a tennis ball and then ask the children what size ball it is. Talk about how they can tell the size by the way you mime it. Call out someone's name and ask the person to catch the ball and throw it back to you.

Now tell the children to stand just outside the circle and throw and catch a small, imaginary ball in pairs until you say stop. After a short while, stop the activity and tell them to throw or bounce a large, imaginary ball to each other. Repeat this process by asking them to play with an imaginary bat and ball, followed by a balloon. Keep these activities short but ask some pairs to demonstrate their mimes if you see any good practice.

Move back into the circle and hold an imaginary mug of hot tea in your hand. Talk about how you might mime passing this to someone, so that it appears to be a mug of hot liquid. Suggest things such as blowing on it and holding it with one hand underneath and one hand on the handle to indicate the size and weight of the mug. Ask the children to mime passing the mug of hot tea around the circle. Then pass a second mug the opposite way round the circle, to see what happens when they meet up.

Next, ask the children to work in pairs, and explain that they will be given an activity to mime. They will be allowed a few minutes to prepare the mime before being asked to perform it to the class. Encourage them to make their mime as interesting as possible and suggest that they include extra things that might happen while carrying out the activity. For example, if they were playing music in a band they might accidentally knock over the music stand. Use the following list to allocate mime sequences to groups of children, who should then work in pairs to practise the mimes. Pairs can work together or as individuals alongside each other:

▲ learning to juggle
▲ making a sandcastle on a beach
▲ making and eating a sandwich
▲ watering plants and weeding a garden
▲ cleaning a bedroom and making a bed
▲ mixing paints and painting a picture
▲ lifting weights and working out in a gym
▲ shovelling snow from a driveway and making a snowman.

Let groups doing the same mimes perform to the others, and point out any good practice.

Give each pair one of the mime cards made from photocopiable pages 128 and 129. Make it clear that pairs should do the same mime sequence alongside each other, but they should plan the mimes together and can interact if they wish. They should use at least some of the ideas on the card but they can also add their own ideas. Stress that the mimes must fit the title on the card and be carried out sensibly. Mimes can be amusing but not silly. Warn the class not to throw themselves around or do anything that could be dangerous when miming.

Give the children a few minutes to read the cards first, before they start working on the mimes. Encourage them to exaggerate the movements to perform a convincing mime. Ask those who finish well before the others to develop and extend their mime sequence, but when two or three pairs have finished, stop the activity.

Now let pairs take turns to read out their titles and perform their mime sequences to the rest of the class. Point out any good practice after each performance and invite the class to pick out the parts they thought were most effectively mimed. Insist on positive comments only. Conclude by talking about what makes a good mime sequence.

Suggestion(s) for extension
Let confident children work together, and encourage them to develop their card sequences into a story in which something happens to cause difficulties.

Suggestion(s) for support
Make alternative mime cards for those pairs who need support. Restrict the wording to one sentence or phrase. Choose broad themes such as playing with a football, doing housework, gardening, juggling, washing up.

Assessment opportunities
Look for children who extend their mimes to include more detail and those who attempt to make their miming accurate.

Performance ideas
The children who have developed and extended their mimed sequences into a story in the extension activity can produce a performance, with the addition of a few costumes and props.

Reference to photocopiable sheets
Photocopiable pages 128 and 129 provide the text for the mime cards used in the final part of the activity.

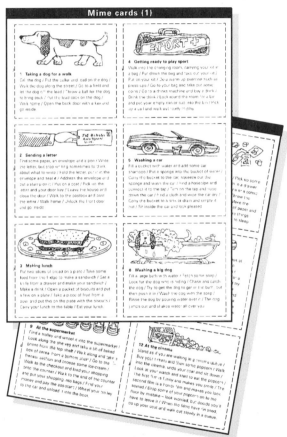

MIME A POEM

To use actions to perform key words or phrases in a poem.

†† _Whole class and pairs._

⏱ _30–45 minutes._

Previous skills/knowledge needed
Children should have read the chosen poem and need to have had some experience of mime work.

Key background information
This activity uses actions and mime to communicate the meanings of individual words in a poem. This includes more

abstract words which encourage children to use mime in a more symbolic way. In searching for an appropriate action, they are also encouraged to think about the exact meaning of the word or phrase within the context of the poem. Performing a poem in this way creates images for the children, which help them to remember the poem and appreciate the richness and depth of the words.

Preparation

Make one copy of photocopiable page 130 per pair. Make a copy of your chosen poem. (You can use a whole poem or part of a poem.) Underline the key nouns and other words or phrases in the poem that could be represented by an action. For example:

The <u>fox</u> <u>crept silently</u>
<u>Along</u> the <u>grassy</u> <u>bank</u>.
His <u>eyes</u> <u>darted quickly</u>,
This way and that,
<u>Looking</u> for his <u>prey</u>.

Then make one copy of the underlined version of the poem for each pair of children. Divide the poem up into sections, with four to six underlined words in each section. Highlight one section on each copy, so that every pair of children has one highlighted section on which to work. If the poem is short, some pairs will inevitably be given the same highlighted sections as other pairs. This will not cause a problem during the activity. You may even want to ensure that this happens in order to support less confident pairs (see 'Suggestion(s) for support').

Resources needed

Copies of your chosen poem, photocopiable page 130, highlighter pen.

What to do

Organize the class into pairs of similar ability and give each pair a copy of photocopiable page 130. Look at section A. Take each word in turn and discuss how to perform an action

to help people understand what the word means. Let children demonstrate their ideas and, if they are appropriate, let all the class try them out. If the children find this difficult, give them a few ideas to start them off, for example by suggesting how the following words could be represented:
▲ rain – run the fingers up and down like falling raindrops
▲ house – draw the shape of a house in the air
▲ funny – pretend to laugh or smile silently
▲ bright – squint the eyes and shield them with the hands
▲ flying – wave arms like a bird
▲ scurried – lean forwards and run on the spot
▲ smoothly – make a stroking movement with the hands
▲ cautiously – look anxiously from side to side.

Now look at sections B, C and D and share out the sentences according to ability. Give each pair one sentence from a particular section. Section B provides the easiest sentences and section D provides the most difficult. Tell each pair to work out an action for all the underlined words in their sentence and then work out actions for some of the other sentences. (Make it clear that both children in the pair should do the same actions.) Ensure that the children have enough room to practise their actions. This may mean asking pairs to work in different parts of the room or moving back the chairs to create room behind the desks. Stress that actions should be simple and should not be boisterous or involve moving across the room. Encourage the children to exaggerate the actions and perform them slowly so that the meaning is communicated effectively.

Stop the activity when most pairs have finished their given sentence. Then let pairs perform their actions as you read the sentences.

Next, give out the highlighted copies of the poem. Read the poem through and then explain that each pair must work out an action for each of the words, or groups of words, that have been highlighted on their copy. Warn the children that they will be asked to perform their actions to the class, as you read the poem. Talk about the meanings of some of the underlined words. Then choose one word from each highlighted section and let the class make brief

DRAMA

suggestions for an appropriate action. Now let the children work out their own actions.

When most pairs have completed the task, rehearse the activity by reading the poem very slowly, while pairs perform the actions. Pause at the end of each section, to make sure that the next set of pairs are ready to come in. Now read the poem without stopping and let the children perform their highlighted sections. Make sure that you read the poem fairly slowly, but without losing the meaning. Repeat this once more so that the children gain confidence in their performance.

Suggestion(s) for extension

Use section D of photocopiable page 130, and highlight longer or more challenging sections of your chosen poem for more confident pairs to perform.

Suggestion(s) for support

Ask less confident children to perform the underlined words in section B of photocopiable page 130. When preparing to perform the poem, give less confident pairs the same highlighted sections as more confident pairs and let them work out the actions for the section as a group of four.

Assessment opportunities

Look for children who understand the meanings of the words within the context of the poem and note those who invent imaginative and appropriate actions. Look for children who are confident in using their bodies to express meaning and those who perform their actions with attention to detail.

Performance ideas

With practice, the poem can be read and performed to a larger audience, using the actions from this activity. Alternatively, children may like to choose all, or part of their own favourite poem, to perform in this way.

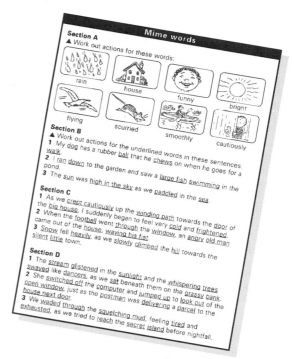

Mime words

Section A
▲ Work out actions for these words:

rain — house — funny — bright

flying — scurried — smoothly — cautiously

Section B
▲ Work out actions for the underlined words in these sentences.
1 My dog has a rubber ball that he chews on when he goes for a walk.
2 I ran down to the garden and saw a large fish swimming in the pond.
3 The sun was high in the sky as we paddled in the sea.

Section C
1 As we crept cautiously up the winding path towards the door of the big house, I suddenly began to feel very cold and frightened.
2 When the football went through the window, an angry old man came out of the house, waving his fist.
3 Snow fell heavily, as we slowly climbed the hill towards the silent little town.

Section D
1 The stream glistened in the sunlight and the whispering trees swayed like dancers, as we sat beneath them on the grassy bank.
2 She switched off the computer and jumped up to look out of the open window, just as the postman was delivering a parcel to the house next door.
3 We waded through the squelching mud, feeling tired and exhausted, as we tried to reach the secret island before nightfall.

Reference to photocopiable sheet

Photocopiable page 130 provides words for the whole class to perform, followed by short sentences for pairs, set at three differentiated levels. These are intended to help children gain confidence in putting actions to words, before they are asked to perform the chosen poem.

THE QUEUE

To develop skills in devising, performing and evaluating a piece of drama.

†† *Small groups performing to the whole class.*

🕒 *45–60 minutes.*

Previous skills/knowledge needed

Children should be able to work co-operatively in small groups.

Key background information

Many children struggle with improvisation, both on a creative and a social level. This activity provides a structure that will both support and extend the children's skills in devising, performing and evaluating a piece of drama.

Preparation

Clear a space in the classroom for a performance area.

Resources needed

Flip chart or board, writing materials, a camera (optional).

What to do

Organize the children into mixed-ability groups, with three to four in each group, and ask the groups to sit in front of the performance area. Make sure that they can also see the board. Choose a confident group to come into the performance area, and ask them to stand in a line, facing the class. Ask the class to imagine that these children are waiting in a queue and have been waiting for a long time. Ask the class to decide why the children are queuing. Tell the children at the front to practise standing still as if someone had taken a photograph of them in the queue. Invite the class to make suggestions about how they would be standing and how they would be feeling. Include suggestions on appropriate facial expressions.

On the word 'Freeze', ask the queue to stand still for a few seconds, as if they were in the photograph. After the photograph has been made, tell the group to relax the freeze and then ask the class what they think might happen if the photograph were to come to life for a few minutes. Focus on what the people might say and how they might behave. Ask the queue to make the photograph again on the word 'Freeze' and then come to life when you say the word 'Action'. Explain that they must keep talking until you say 'Freeze' once more. Let this go on for a maximum of about 30 seconds to a minute, or less, if the children run out of things to say. Make sure the queue receives some applause from the class before they sit down.

Explain to the children that their task will be to work in their groups to prepare a similar improvisation entitled 'The queue', but explain that they must choose a different situation from the one that has just been demonstrated. Discuss some ideas and write a list of possibilities on the board, for example queuing for a bus or a fairground ride,

or queuing to see a pop concert or a film. Each group should choose one of the situations. Before the children start the task, give them the following five rules as guidelines:

1 The improvisation must last between one and two minutes.
2 Everyone in the group must be given a reasonable speaking part.
3 The work must start and finish with a 'frozen' photograph position.
4 The actors can say anything, so long as it makes sense in the situation and is not rude or silly. No one should say anything that could upset anyone else.
5 In the interests of safety there should be no physical contact or dangerous stunts.

Ask them to try to make the improvisations interesting in some way by making them intriguing, tense or amusing. Discuss some possibilities and write these on the board.

Now let the groups work on their improvisations. Encourage groups to choose their situation within the first few minutes. This will ensure that all the groups will have enough time to spend on devising and rehearsing. It is not advisable to spend too long with any one group. Resist any invitations to watch everything a group has done so far. Just ask them to show you the part that is causing them a problem, and make suggestions on how to solve it. Focus on those groups who need support to make decisions or come to agreements. If any group should finish well before the others, encourage them to add something else to their work to make it even better.

When you are satisfied that all the groups can make a reasonable attempt at an improvisation, stop the class. Explain that everyone will now have a final word rehearsal. When you say 'Action', every group must start their word rehearsal, and when they have finished they should fold their arms and wait in silence for any groups who have still to finish. Warn them that you will have to stop any group who goes on longer than two minutes. If a group has a bad rehearsal, allow the other groups some extra rehearsal time while you help the struggling group(s).

Now let each group perform to the rest of the class. Each group must start their improvisation by making an imaginary photograph. (Real photographs can be taken if you want to record the moments for a display.) Tell the children that the queue must come to life when you say 'Action'. Tell each group to finish their improvisation by holding the last photograph for a few seconds before

relaxing. Make sure each group receives a round of applause after their performance.

After each improvisation, ask the class to pick out what they liked best about the performance. Discourage any negative comments about the acting by explaining that you are trying to build up their confidence. After the children have made their observations, use the opportunity to point out examples of good drama practice, such as making the characters believable; using contrast, tension or humour; remembering what to say; facing the audience; speaking clearly. Try to point out something positive about every improvisation.

Suggestion(s) for extension
Confident children may like to script their improvisations for a class book of plays. Scripted improvisations can be given to other groups to perform, to see if any stage directions are needed before being put into the class book.

Suggestion(s) for support
As you move around the groups, make sure that the less confident children can remember what they want to say. Help them think of simple sentences that you know they will remember. If a child is unwilling or unable to speak in an improvisation, suggest that he or she makes a non-verbal contribution, such as pacing up and down looking at his or her watch. Alternatively, ask the child to play the part of the photographer, who takes the first and last pictures of each group, either real or imagined.

Assessment opportunities
Assess children's confidence and skill in working collaboratively in a group situation and speaking and performing in front of an audience. Note any examples of individual creativity and imagination. Inviting the children to respond to the drama creates an opportunity to assess the extent to which they understand and appreciate drama as an art form.

Opportunities for IT
Let some children use a word processor to write and present scripted versions of their improvisations. They can use published scripts as models. If the school has access to a digital camera, or can scan conventional photographs, these digital images can be included in the scripts to show the queue in the first moment at the start of the action and then in the final moment.

The children could also use a word processor to write summaries of each improvisation for display purposes.

Performance ideas
Let groups perform a script written by another group.

Display ideas
Scripted improvisations can be included in a class book of plays and placed with other reading materials or hung on a wall. Drawings of the photographs or the real photographs can be displayed, together with brief summaries of each improvisation. (See 'Opportunities for IT'.)

ONE MINUTE ON

To use a picture as a stimulus for small group improvisations.

†† *Small groups performing to the whole class.*

⏱ *Session One: 45–60 minutes. Session Two: 30–45 minutes.*

Previous skills/knowledge needed
Children should be able to work co-operatively in small groups and should be familiar with the concept of spoken thoughts and making freeze-frames (see 'Significant moments' on page 18).

Key background information
This activity is designed around interpretations of a given image as a stimulus for drama. It is divided into two sessions, which can be carried out in one long session if you wish. The activity is used to stimulate small group improvisation work, but it can also support other subject areas, according to the nature of the still image. Famous paintings can be explored in this way in an art lesson, and old photographs can be researched and brought to life in a history lesson.

Preparation
Clear an acting area and place a table and four chairs in the area. Make one copy of photocopiable page 131 per child.

Resources needed
An acting area, a table and four chairs, photocopiable page 131, writing materials, a large copy or several small copies

of a painting or a photograph (choose an image that contains a number of people).

What to do
Session One

Organize the class into mixed-ability groups of four, ideally made up of two boys and two girls. (Use groups of three if the numbers don't work out for fours.) Ask the children to sit in their groups, facing the acting area, and give each child a copy of photocopiable page 131. Invite one group of children to come into the acting area to make a freeze-frame of the picture on the sheet. Encourage them to make the freeze-frame as visually accurate as possible in terms of where and how the people are positioned. Go through each character in turn and discuss what they might be thinking at this moment. Tell all the children to fill in their version of the thought bubbles on the sheet and then start to fill in the ideas about what might happen during the next minute.

When everyone has filled in the thought bubbles, collect some ideas about what might happen if the picture came alive for one minute. Talk about how each idea might be acted out and what a second picture might look like after one minute. Demonstrate one or two ideas for final pictures by asking a few children to make freeze-frames.

Tell the class to talk about their ideas in groups and then work out a piece of drama to show what happened when the picture was brought to life for about one minute. Explain that each group must start with a freeze-frame of the original picture and when one of the group says 'Action', they must

come to life. They must also finish on a freeze-frame when one of the group says 'Freeze'. Give them some rules for improvising (see the rules used in 'The queue' on page 46).

When the groups have finished their improvisations they should perform them to another group, who should time them. Anything less than a minute or longer than two minutes should be adjusted.

After the children have finished devising and rehearsing their improvisations, ask them to sit in front of the acting area and let groups perform to the class. After each performance, ask the group to pick out the parts they think worked best and any parts they would most like to improve. Then ask the class to pick out the thing they liked best about the piece. After the performances, go back to the photocopiable sheets and ask each child to write a few sentences about what happened in their drama.

Session Two

Show the class the painting or the photograph and talk about who the people might be, where they are and why they might be there. Talk about what they might be feeling and what might happen if the picture were brought to life for about one minute and then frozen again. Tell the children to work in their groups, as in Session One, and use the picture to start off a short improvisation as before. Remind the class to start and stop with a freeze. Let groups perform their improvisations to the rest of the class, as in Session One. Point out how the same stimulus can produce a number of different stories for drama.

Suggestion(s) for extension

Ask more confident children to write a scripted version of their improvisation, after writing the summary on the photocopiable sheet at the end of Session One. In Session Two, ask more confident children to make up an improvisation showing what happened the minute before the event in the painting or photograph. They should finish their improvisation with a freeze-frame depicting the image in the painting or photograph.

Suggestion(s) for support

Allow less confident children to work with a partner to fill in a copy of photocopiable page 131 in Session One. Encourage less confident children to be realistic about what they choose to say in the improvisations. Listen in to the groups as they are devising and check that less confident children feel secure about what they have to say in the improvisation. Alternatively, put less confident children into one group and help them to create a freeze-frame version of 'One minute on'.

Assessment opportunities

Look for children who make progress from Session One to Session Two. Note those who are able to develop, explain

and share ideas and opinions and look for those who are confident when performing to an audience.

Opportunities for IT

In Session Two, let some children use an encyclopaedia CD-ROM to look for information about the famous painting that will be used in the drama. If the school has access to the Internet they may be able to find information there as well. In both activities children will need to be shown how to set up a search and follow option to locate the information needed. They may also need to be shown how to print the information or to save it to disk.

Performance ideas

Some of the improvisations can be developed and rehearsed to perform to a wider audience.

Display ideas

Background information about the chosen painting or photograph can be printed out and put on display alongside sketches made by children of their version of the picture 'One minute on'. These sketches can be based on the final freeze-frames used in the improvisations.

Reference to photocopiable sheet

Photocopiable page 131 provides a simple picture for the children to use as a stimulus for a piece of improvisation. This helps them gain confidence in the process before attempting to use a real painting or photograph, which could be more complicated.

START HERE

To create small group improvisations from a given first line.

†† *Small groups performing to the whole class.*

🕐 *45–60 minutes.*

Previous skills/knowledge needed

Children should be able to work co-operatively in small groups. They should have some prior experience of working on simple improvisations.

Key background information

When children work on improvisations they often spend all their time deciding how to start. This activity will help the children move straight into their improvisations by giving them a first line. The lines suggest moments of tension which can be followed through in the improvisation.

Preparation

Ensure that the groups have enough room to practise their improvisations. Make two copies of photocopiable page 132, mount the sheets onto thin card and cover them with clear self-adhesive plastic film. Cut out the sentences to make 20 cards.

Resources needed

An acting area, photocopiable page 132, two sheets of thin A4 card, adhesive, clear self-adhesive plastic film, scissors, rough paper, writing materials.

What to do

Organize the class into small mixed-ability groups, with three to four in each group. Give each group a card and explain that they are going to carry out a short improvisation which starts with someone saying the line on the card. Take the first card as an example and collect some ideas on how to build a story around this line for an improvisation.

Once the children have understood the task, tell them that they have up to ten minutes to plan an outline for their improvisation, working in their groups. Encourage them to

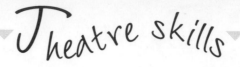

make brief notes and tell them to let you know when they have a plan. Make sure that everyone is well on the way to making a decision about the storyline after ten minutes.

When you are satisfied with a group's plan, let the children work out the improvisation practically. Make it clear that groups can adapt their original plans if they need to. Encourage groups to work at improving their improvisations in the same way as they would draft a piece of writing. If any groups still finish well before the others, give them another card to work on.

When most groups have finished, ask everyone to have a final rehearsal and then call the children together in front of the acting area. Let each group perform their improvisation to the class. Point out any differences in the way identical lines might have been developed. Ask the children to respond to each improvisation by picking out the parts they liked best. Ask children to focus on positive comments and encourage them to back up their opinions by referring to specific examples in the performances.

Suggestion(s) for extension

Give more confident groups two cards. Ask them to start or finish with one of the lines and include the other line somewhere in the middle of the improvisation. Encourage them to explore the effects of contrast, by alternating moments of tension with moments of light relief in their work.

Suggestion(s) for support

Put less confident children in groups with those who are likely to support and include them. Observe less confident children closely when they are working in their groups and intervene if necessary to offer support. Encourage them to choose speaking parts that they are happy with and can cope with. Support children who are unwilling or unable to play a speaking part, by suggesting an appropriate non-speaking part.

Assessment opportunities

Look for children who are able to explore and develop their own ideas and extend ideas offered by others. Look for those who are able to structure and develop a piece of improvisation with the audience in mind. Note any children who are confident and convincing when they are playing a sensitive role.

Performance ideas

Some of the improvisations can be rehearsed to be performed to a wider audience.

Display ideas

Ask each group to produce a storyboard sequence of their improvisation for a display. The first frame should incorporate their first line (either as text or as a visual image).

Reference to photocopiable sheet

Photocopiable page 132 provides the text for ten cards containing lines to start separate improvisations. Children can keep their cards to refer to while working. Using cards encourages them to persevere with the line they have been allocated; if they are given the whole sheet they may find it tempting to look down the list of lines for an easier one.

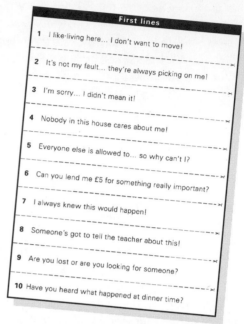

First lines

1 I like living here... I don't want to move!

2 It's not my fault... they're always picking on me!

3 I'm sorry... I didn't mean it!

4 Nobody in this house cares about me!

5 Everyone else is allowed to... so why can't I?

6 Can you lend me £5 for something really important?

7 I always knew this would happen!

8 Someone's got to tell the teacher about this!

9 Are you lost or are you looking for someone?

10 Have you heard what happened at dinner time?

ENTRANCES

To develop confidence in starting an improvisation with a non-verbal activity.

†† *Small groups performing to the whole class.*

🕑 *30–45 minutes.*

Previous skills/knowledge needed

Children should be able to work co-operatively in groups and should have had some prior experience in working out simple improvisations.

Key background information

This activity is an attempt to introduce children to the potential of non-verbal entrances to engage the audience, instead of going straight into dialogue. Children often find it difficult to maintain silences during an improvisation, believing that the power lies in keeping the dialogue going. This activity focuses on maintaining interest through 30 seconds of silence at the beginning of each improvisation. Consequently, the content of the improvisations in this activity is of less importance than the quality of the entrances and this should be conveyed to the children.

Preparation

Make two copies of photocopiable page 133, mount them onto thin card, cover them with clear self-adhesive plastic film and cut out the 16 cards.

Resources needed

A large space, a whistle, photocopiable page 133, two sheets of thin A4 card, adhesive, self-adhesive clear plastic film, scissors, paper, writing materials.

What to do

Organize the children into small mixed-ability groups, with three in each group. Explain that the purpose of this activity is to look at non-verbal ways of holding the attention of the audience at the start of an improvisation. Tell the children that each group will be given a card explaining what should happen at the start of their improvisation. The card will describe the first 30 seconds of the drama, which should be acted in silence. The challenge will be to make this section interesting for the audience, using actions and facial expressions. Explain that the timing is only approximate but after about 30 seconds of silence, the actors should start to speak. Tell the children that they won't be expected to finish their improvisation, as they will be concentrating on the 30-second entrance and how the speaking is introduced.

Take one of the cards and read it to the class as an example. Ask the class to give you ideas on what the actors could do to keep the attention of the audience for 30 seconds, without speaking. Write their ideas down in note form on a sheet of paper. Ask the class to suggest an order of events and number the events accordingly. Tell the children to find a space and let them all act out the suggestions, as you read them.

Gather the children together but ask them to sit in their groups. Give one card and one sheet of paper to each group. Tell them to write down ideas for what the actors could do and number them in order, as you did previously. When groups have completed this, they should show you the paper and then practise the entrance and the first few lines of spoken dialogue. Make it clear that everyone in the group must take part in the entrance scene. Explain that if you want to speak to the whole class, you will blow the whistle for them to stop. Go round the groups and encourage them to focus on developing the entrance scene rather than the rest of the drama.

When most groups appear to have been through their ideas at least once, blow the whistle and stop the work.

Call the class together and ask each group to show the class their work so far. Ask the class to help each group by making suggestions for improvements. Then ask the groups to consider the suggestions made by the class as they resume work on their improvisations. When most groups have moved on to the speaking parts, blow the whistle and call the class together.

Now let groups perform to each other. After each performance, ask the class to pick out the things they thought worked best in the entrance scenes. Encourage them to use silent moments when devising other improvisations in the future.

Suggestion(s) for extension

Encourage more confident groups to create another opportunity for silence, within the development of the drama. Suggest a moment such as waiting for an important phone call or for someone to call at the house, or a moment when someone is hiding and another actor is pottering about but getting close to discovering the hidden person by accident.

Suggestion(s) for support

Put less confident children in groups with those who will accept and include them. Ensure that less confident children are given parts that will challenge them, while making sure that they can cope.

Assessment opportunities

Look for children who are willing and able to work on the non-verbal activities in detail. Note those who are able to put feelings across using mime and facial expressions. Look for children who are able to offer imaginative and appropriate ideas within a group and those who take the initiative during moments of indecision.

Performance ideas

Some of this work can be developed into full improvisations, particularly if groups have incorporated other moments of silence within the rest of the drama. These can be performed to the rest of the class as examples of silences within the development of a drama, as well as at the start.

Reference to photocopiable sheet

Photocopiable page 133 provides the text for a number of cards, outlining different situations for silent entrances. These situation cards can be referred to by the groups as they are working.

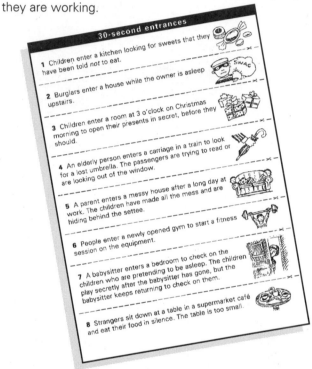

30-second entrances

1 Children enter a kitchen looking for sweets that they have been told *not* to eat.

2 Burglars enter a house while the owner is asleep upstairs.

3 Children enter a room at 3 o'clock on Christmas morning to open their presents in secret, before they should.

4 An elderly person enters a carriage in a train to look for a lost umbrella. The passengers are trying to read or are looking out of the window.

5 A parent enters a messy house after a long day at work. The children have made all the mess and are hiding behind the settee.

6 People enter a newly opened gym to start a fitness session on the equipment.

7 A babysitter enters a bedroom to check on the children who are pretending to be asleep. The children play secretly after the babysitter has gone, but the babysitter keeps returning to check on them.

8 Strangers sit down at a table in a supermarket café and eat their food in silence. The table is too small.

ADVERTS

To give children an opportunity to perform in the style of television or radio advertising.

†† *Small groups performing to the whole class.*

🕐 *Session One: 45–60 minutes. Session Two: 45–60 minutes.*

Previous skills/knowledge needed

The children should be familiar with a range of TV and radio adverts. They should have had an opportunity to analyse the genre at a simple level prior to this activity. The children should also be able to work co-operatively in groups.

Key background information

This activity provides an opportunity to look at how drama can be used to persuade and influence people. In identifying

and mimicking advertising styles, the children will become more aware of the power of media advertising as a genre in its own right. The adverts produced by the children are intended to be versions of existing styles, so the children should be encouraged to recall and reflect on advertisements they have seen and heard in the media. It may be easier to concentrate on adverts using storylines or events.

This activity is divided into two sessions, which should ideally be separated by no longer than a week. Session Two encourages the children to subvert the genre in order to make the adverts amusing. This requires them to use their powers of persuasion and skills in performance to sell a totally new and highly unlikely kind of product.

Preparation

Make a space for the groups to practise acting out the adverts. Write four imaginary advertising slogans on separate A4 cards. Make up your own or use the following:

Traveller's Instant Coffee, for the taste that takes you further.
Harrison's Headache Tablets, for the quiet life.
Washo Washing Powder... the powder that washes everything clean.
Moonlight Crunchies... the biscuits that go crunch in the night.

Make two copies per group of photocopiable page 134.

Resources needed

Space for each group to practise their advert, four A4 cards, writing materials, flip chart or board, photocopiable page 134, one pair of sunglasses or enough pairs to give one to each group.

What to do

Session One

Organize the class into small mixed-ability groups, with three to four in each group. Talk about the children's favourite and least favourite adverts on TV and encourage the class to analyse why they like or dislike them.

Show the children the advertising slogans and explain that each group will be asked to prepare and perform a TV advert for one of the products. The advert should last between 30 seconds and a minute. Discuss some possibilities for each one. Ask the children to make their advert similar to those that they have seen or heard in the media.

Consider the kind of persuasive vocabulary used in TV advertising and write a list on the board of words and phrases that the children decide are those most commonly used for persuasion. Ask the children to incorporate some of these words into their own adverts. Make it clear that amusing versions will be acceptable, providing they are tasteful and safe.

Decide on the product that each group will work on and give out one copy of photocopiable page 134 per group to help them plan their work. Ask the groups to show you their completed sheet before they start working practically, but stress that these plans can be changed if they do not work out as well as expected. When most groups have finished, call the children together in front of the acting area and let them perform their adverts to each other.

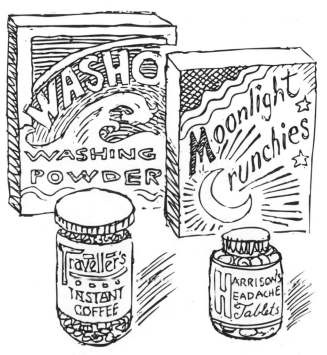

Session Two

Ask the groups to make up and perform a TV advert based on a new invention. The invention is a pair of glasses that act as a disguise for sleeping through boring lessons or when listening to people talking about boring things. The glasses make you look awake and interested even when you are asleep. Talk about how these might work and how they could be advertised.

Give out a second copy per group of photocopiable page 134 for the children to fill in before they start acting out their adverts. Distribute the sunglasses as props. If you only have one pair of sunglasses, then explain that these will be given to groups to use during the final performances. When most groups have completed their improvisations, let them perform to each other.

Suggestion(s) for extension

During Session One, ask more confident groups to work out a radio version of their TV advert. Simple percussion instruments may be used for jingles or sound effects, as long as they don't disturb other groups.

Suggestion(s) for support

Differentiate through questioning during the initial discussions, to encourage less confident children to talk about their likes and dislikes concerning TV adverts. Put less confident children in groups with those who will support and include them and make sure that they are given suitable parts that will enable them to succeed.

Assessment opportunities

Look for children who show an understanding of the styles and approaches used in TV adverts and note those children who are able to use and extend the suggested persuasive vocabulary in their adverts. Look for children who adapt their role-play to suit the genre.

Opportunities for IT

Children could use an art or drawing package to create an advert for their product, incorporating pictures. It could even include a World Wide Web address and be similar to an Internet style advert. This would require them to have looked at different sorts of advertising on the Internet to understand the style as well as its limitations.

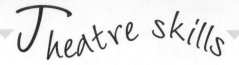

Performance ideas

Any radio versions can be played or performed to the class, and the TV adverts can be polished up and rehearsed to a standard suitable for performing to a wider audience.

Display ideas

The magazine adverts (see 'Opportunities for IT') can be displayed along with some examples of real-life advertising from magazines.

Reference to photocopiable sheet

Photocopiable page 134 provides a writing frame which encourages groups to discuss possibilities and plan their adverts, before they start to act them out.

Advert planning sheet

Name _____ Date _____

Ideas for the advert	The best idea

Characters in the advert and who will play them
(Choose at least one character for each member of your group.)

1 _____

2 _____

3 _____

4 _____

▲ How will your advert start?

▲ How will your advert end?

▲ What persuasive words will you use?

ACTING IN THE SCHOOL PLAY

To build confidence in performing a play in front of a larger audience.

†† *Whole class and/or small groups.*

🕐 *Six sessions: 30–45 minutes per session.*

Previous skills/knowledge needed

The children should be familiar with the storyline or sequence of events in the chosen play. They should know who will be playing which characters. Select children to play the characters based on your knowledge of individual children – this is better than holding lengthy auditions. It is important that a child isn't asked to play a part that he or she does not feel happy with.

Key background information

These activities provide a range of ideas for rehearsing plays of different kinds at different levels. They are organized in sessions which are broadly progressive, but select those activities which suit the needs of your particular group and the play you are using. Look through published plays carefully to make sure they are suitable and adapt them if necessary. Sometimes it is easier to devise your own play from children's own improvisations on a particular theme. Work of this nature is often easier for the children to remember. They also feel a sense of ownership over the material, which gives them greater confidence when performing.

You may want to integrate children's improvised material into the dialogue of a published play, so that you can work within a ready-made structure. Whatever the method, make sure that the children can cope with the demands of the dialogue. Choose plays with parts for as many children as possible and avoid those which rely too heavily on one central character. Choose plays with strong but simple storylines which will hold the interest of both the audience and the cast. If children are interested in the play they will concentrate better during rehearsals. Plays adapted from popular children's novels are excellent for maintaining interest and will also encourage children to make comparisons between the two genres.

Preparation

Divide your chosen play into small sections – these are known as rehearsal units – involving one main event or scene per unit. Mark these units off on a master script and give each unit a number. Make enough copies of

photocopiable page 135 to cover your rehearsal units and fill in the grids. Make one copy of photocopiable page 136 for each character in the play. Prepare a space for the rehearsals. Write out a short, scene-by-scene summary of the main events in the play, focusing on what the characters do rather than what they feel. Write each character's name on a separate Post-It note.

Resources needed

A playscript, a space for rehearsals, photocopiable pages 135 and 136, a small pad of Post-It notes, paper, writing materials, a few spare chairs.

What to do
Session One

Read an outline summary of your chosen play to remind the children of what happens in the play. Using the prepared Post-It notes, ask each child to wear the name label for their character. Slowly read out the summary of the first scene and let the characters walk through the events, according to what you say is happening. The characters should not speak, but they can mime if they wish. Warn the children that there may be moments when they are immobile. Don't spend time making the scene accurate, just concentrate on making sure the right characters move at the right times.

Session Two

Read through the scene or section of the play that is being rehearsed. Ask the children to pick out what they feel is the most important moment, or moments, in that section. Limit the number of moments to three. Let them stage each moment as if it were a 'frozen' moment on a video (see 'Significant moments' on page 18).

Discuss where the characters might be placed in relation to each other and in relation to the audience. Discuss what each character might be thinking and feeling at that moment and encourage the characters to reflect it in their facial

Explain to the class that this is rather like a silent movie in the sense that everything happens quickly. Let the characters walk through each scene in the play, according to your summary. Keep the activity light-hearted. Children are likely to be a little confused on the first attempt and mistakes should be expected.

Repeat the activity again, so that the children begin to anticipate where to stand and what to do. This will help them to gain a sense of the whole play and give them confidence. If the activity is fun it will provide a positive start to rehearsing the play.

expressions and body posture. Focus on how the characters can best communicate how they are feeling to the audience.

Tell the characters to make the still image when you say the word 'Freeze' and ask the characters to hold the moment to the count of three before relaxing. Ask those who are observing for their comments. This will help the children to think about the characters and the themes in the play in more depth, and to focus their thinking on how to communicate these things to an audience. The emphasis in this activity should be on communication, as much as on analysis and exploration.

Session Three

Focus on one rehearsal unit or scene from the play. Ask one of the characters to sit in a chair facing the class. This is known as the hot-seat. The child playing the character must remain in role for as long as he or she is in the chair. Ask the class to spend a few minutes working in pairs to make up at least two questions to ask the character. Children should ask questions as themselves, not as other characters in the play.

Make it clear to the children that they are focusing on a particular point in the play when questioning the character. You should decide whether they are talking to the character before or after a particular scene or somewhere in the middle of it. Encourage the children to ask questions that will help everyone understand how the character feels, rather than irrelevant questions such as 'What is your favourite colour?'

Act as a chairperson to keep the session on task and ask questions yourself if necessary. Keep each individual hot-seating session fairly brief. Let all the characters in the rehearsal unit or scene have an opportunity to sit on the hot-seat. Minor characters can be hot-seated as a group, if this is more convenient.

After each hot-seat, ask the children what they have found out about that character's personality. Give each child a copy of photocopiable page 136 and ask them to fill in section A on their character's personality.

Session Four

Select one of the main characters in your rehearsal unit and ask the child playing that character to sit in a chair facing the group. Give the children a few minutes to think about what their own characters think and feel about the character in the chair, at this particular point in the play. (They should talk about this in pairs to help each other.)

Ask the child on the chair to consider what his or her

character thinks about each of the other characters in turn, but explain that he or she will be given help with this during the activity. Ask this child to start by identifying who the character that he or she is playing likes best and who the character likes least. Keep this part of the activity very brief.

Then go round each character in turn and invite them to say what they think and feel about the central character at this point in the play. If they find this difficult, ask the group to make suggestions. Then ask the central character what he or she thinks about the other characters. Make suggestions yourself and invite the group to speculate on this. Repeat this process with each of the characters to explore their relationships with the central character at this point in the play.

Conclude the activity by asking each child to fill in what other characters think of their character, in section B on a copy of photocopiable page 136.

Session Five

This can be a whole-class activity relating to the whole play or one relating to a particular rehearsal unit. The activity requires enough space for the characters to move around.

Tell the children to find a space. Ask them to walk around the room as their normal selves and as if they are alone (on the word 'Action'). They should do this until you say the word 'Freeze', when they should stop. Then ask them to walk again, but this time they should walk as if they were their character. Tell them to think about their character's personality and how this might be communicated to the audience in the way that the character walks and moves. Give the children a few seconds to think about how their character would walk, before they start.

Repeat the activity using different situations and feelings each time, such as walking as if their character is in a hurry, walking along a beach, feeling angry, feeling bored, feeling happy and so on. Then ask the characters to walk around

and greet the other characters by saying 'Hello' in a voice their character might use. Encourage them to try different voices as they move around, until they find a voice they are happy with. Some children may find this difficult and should not worry if they cannot put on a different voice. Characters should greet everyone as if they were just being polite. Remind the children to walk in character as they move around.

Now ask the group to sit facing a small acting area. Ask each child in turn to walk into the acting area as their character. Explain that when they come to the centre they should stop and use their character's voice to say: 'Hello my name is…' Encourage each child to speak in a clear voice and to look just above the audience's heads as they speak. If numbers and time allow, let each child try this twice.

This activity can be repeated later, using a few lines that the children have learned instead of the greeting being used. Remind the children to use these movements and voices whenever they rehearse.

Session Six

This activity works best when children have started to learn their lines for the play. If they have not already done so, ask the children to highlight their lines on their script. Select a rehearsal unit or scene as the focus for this activity.

Divide the group in half and position them on opposite sides of the room, with their scripts. Ask each child in turn to say or read out a short line from their script, so that the children across the room can hear. Talk about the power of pauses in the lines and encourage the children to read their lines slightly slower than in real life and to hold the pauses slightly longer. Explain how this helps people sitting far away to hear every word. Encourage the actors to look just above the heads of the opposite group as they speak.

After each child has read their line, ask the children on the opposite side of the room to repeat the line, like an echo. If there is a discrepancy, the child should try saying the line again a little slower or louder. Give each child a maximum of three attempts to get the echo right, before moving on to the next child. Choose children from different sides of the room each time, to alternate the echo. This can be adapted to help children practise speaking longer passages of script to an audience, without the echo.

Give children as many opportunities as possible to learn their lines by earmarking small units of time for the task at various moments during the school day. Assign a lines partner to each child so that they become familiar with each other's lines and can help each other to learn them.

Suggestion(s) for extension

Put more confident children into small groups and ask them to act out a short scene to show how their characters might react in situations other than those in the play. Choose moments of tension such as becoming stuck in a lift or stuck in a tunnel on a train. Other situations might include becoming lost in a forest or trapped in a castle. They should act in character and respond to each other as they would in the play.

Suggestion(s) for support

Make sure that less confident children are given parts that they are happy with and feel they can cope with. If children are unable or unwilling to play speaking parts, invite them to play non-speaking parts. If there are no such parts in the script, invent extra characters with non-speaking parts, such as onlookers, neighbours, servants, friends or people bringing written messages.

If children are reluctant to play a part of any kind, ask them to be advisers to the director and ask for their opinions and help in rehearsals. Supplement this role by giving them stagehand tasks with responsibility, such as collecting the small props after each rehearsal to keep in a box. These should then be put out on a special props table before each rehearsal. (Place small props on a table covered with white paper and draw around each prop with a pencil, so that it is easy to see if any are missing.)

Give support to less confident children who have speaking parts by giving them a more confident lines partner and providing them with plenty of opportunities to practise.

Assessment opportunities

Look for children who are confident when performing in front of an audience and who are able to memorize and deliver their lines with expression. Note any children who make perceptive comments about the characters and relationships within the play and those who respond imaginatively when discussing the events. Look for children who are supportive of others and work for the good of the play as a whole.

Display ideas

The completed character profiles on copies of photocopiable page 136 can be displayed along with photographs taken during the initial rehearsals.

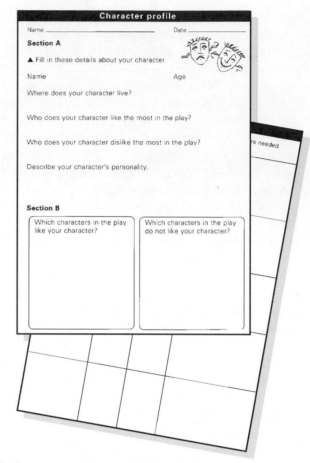

Reference to photocopiable sheets

Photocopiable page 135 provides a grid for you to help plan the rehearsals. Photocopiable page 136 provides a writing frame to encourage each child to build up a personality for their character. This will help them to decide how to play the character when acting.

MAKING A RESPONSE

To encourage children to make constructive responses to drama they have watched.

†† *Whole class and small groups.*

🕓 *Session One: 15–20 minutes. Session Two: 45–60 minutes.*

Previous skills/knowledge needed

Children should know the title of the play they are to watch and be shown pictures of different types of theatre and staging. They should be familiar with basic theatre vocabulary such as 'actors', 'stage', 'curtains', 'set', 'costume', 'props', 'scene', 'special effects', 'interval' and 'spotlight'.

Key background information

This activity is designed to be used after children have been given the opportunity to see a theatrical performance, and it is intended to complement ongoing attempts to develop their critical awareness of theatre. Children should gradually be introduced to a theatre vocabulary in the context of their own performance work. Terms such as 'audience' and 'actors' should be used whenever children perform to each other, along with other vocabulary when appropriate, for example 'narrator', 'costume', 'script', 'lines', 'stage area'. Children should also be made aware of other aspects of acting and performance when you point out good practice in their own work.

Listening to comments on their own performances will enable children to become familiar with what to look for in a theatrical play. This will help them to develop a theatrical vocabulary with which to discuss and respond to drama performed by others. Look for opportunities to extend children's vocabulary by using phrases such as 'projecting the voice', 'facing the audience', 'keeping in character', 'developing facial expressions', 'using contrast and tension', 'using a narrator', 'using props to good effect' and 'using accurate mime'.

Preparation

Organize a suitable theatrical performance for the children to watch. Make one copy per child of photocopiable page 137. Set up a cassette player to record the children's voices for the tape-recording activity later.

Resources needed

Photocopiable page 137, writing materials, a cassette player with a built-in microphone and a blank tape.

What to do
Session One

One or two days before the children are due to watch the performance, distribute copies of photocopiable page 137. Ask them to speculate on what their answers might be to some of the questions, then collect in the photocopiable sheets. Explain that they will be asked to answer the questions when they have seen the performance. This will help to focus the children's minds during the performance.

Session Two

After seeing the performance, hold a general discussion about everyone's reaction to the play. Then give the class a few minutes to think about what they liked best and least about the play and why. Stress that there are no right or wrong answers.

Next, ask the children to talk to the person sitting next to them to find out if they have similar or different opinions. Ask those pairs who had similar opinions to identify themselves by putting up their hands, and ask some of these pairs for their opinions. Then ask some of the pairs who had different opinions to speak about where they differed. Now ask probing questions to extend the children's thinking by asking their opinions on other aspects mentioned on the photocopiable sheet that have not yet been covered.

Now ask the class to imagine that they were approached by a presenter from a local radio station as they were coming out of the theatre in groups, after watching the play. Explain that you will play the part of the presenter who will ask them what they thought of the play. Tell the class that you intend to record this onto an audio cassette as if it were a live radio broadcast and will play it back for them to listen to later.

In preparation for this, put the children into mixed-ability groups of three and ask them to help each other to decide on what to say on the tape. Make it clear that everyone will be asked to express an opinion, and ask the groups to make their responses as interesting and varied as possible. When the children are ready, call them out a group at a time to the cassette player to record their interview. Each interview should be kept very brief. Ask the class to be silent while you record each group.

When each group has been interviewed, give out copies of photocopiable page 137 once more and ask the children to write answers to the questions on a separate sheet. When the children have finished their answers, let them listen to the tape.

Suggestion(s) for extension
In the radio interview, ask confident children probing questions that require a more detailed analysis of the play, when being answered. Did they think that the play had a particular message or point to make? See if they can pick out the most important moments of the play.

Suggestion(s) for support
When you are the radio presenter, differentiate through questioning, such as 'How did you feel when…?' or 'Did you feel scared or did you think it was funny when…?' Let the children work in pairs to complete their answers, or prepare a simpler sheet concentrating on favourite parts and least favourite parts of the play.

Assessment opportunities
Look for children who use appropriate vocabulary when discussing the play and who express an opinion, giving valid reasons for their views. Note any children who are able to pick out significant details about the content of the play and the way it was staged.

Opportunities for IT
Let some children write a critical review of the play on a word processor, as if it were in a local newspaper.

Children could also create a simple questionnaire about the play, identifying key questions to ask and recording the responses from the class. These could be stored in a database or spreadsheet and the results presented graphically.

Display ideas
Display any posters or programmes about the play, with the children's review sheets and critical reviews printed out (see 'Opportunities for IT').

Reference to photocopiable sheet
Photocopiable page 137 provides a framework to help the children write a simple critical review of the play.

Personal and social development

Drama often relies on social co-operation and interaction, and children's existing drama skills can be built on and reinforced through the activities in this chapter which promote children's personal and social development. This chapter also includes a short section on using drama games to foster group co-operation. Such games are useful for helping new groups get to know each other, and to help children to bond together as a cohesive group.

Drama activities can be employed to support children's personal and social development in a number of ways. Drama can be useful when exploring moral dilemmas and sensitive issues such as bullying and prejudice. The dramatic context provides a safety net for children to explore and discuss such issues. This chapter uses a number of diverse contexts and situations for this purpose, including an imaginary jury, a magazine problem page, a community of reluctant immigrants and a group of circus performers faced with a moral dilemma.

Other activities use whole-group drama to encourage skills of co-operation and negotiation. Whole-group drama can support children's social development by creating new and more positive relationships within the group. Children who lack confidence can be given roles which demand respect and carry responsibility. Some whole-group drama activities also relate to more specific areas of personal and social development, such as creating a health centre and making laws for a new settlement.

THE JURY

To use hot-seating and role-play to stimulate discussion and debate.

†† *Whole class and groups.*

🕐 *45–60 minutes.*

Previous skills/knowledge needed

The children should understand the term 'jury'. Some previous experience of hot-seating would be helpful, though not essential.

Key background information

Other examples of moral dilemmas can be used instead of, or in addition to, the one used in this activity. Jo can be taken to be a boy or a girl.

Preparation

Make one copy per child of photocopiable page 138.

Resources needed

Photocopiable page 138, writing materials, one empty chair.

What to do

Ask the class to act as a jury in an imaginary court. Explain that the jury will be deciding whether someone's actions were right or wrong, rather than deciding on a guilty or not guilty verdict as in a criminal court. Give each child a copy of photocopiable page 138 and read through section A. Make sure everyone understands the situation given on the sheet. Then read out the statements in section B without comment and ask the children to think about them as they listen. They should not discuss these statements or share their views with others at this stage.

Now read out the statements again, one at a time, and ask the children to mark them according to their views. Make it clear that they will be allowed to change their views later if they wish. Go through the statements a final time and invite the children to say why they marked them in the way they did.

Tell the class that they will be given the chance to interview some of the people who are featured in the situation given on the photocopiable sheet before being asked to make the final decision on whether Jo did the right thing. Explain that you will play the part of one of Amy and Jo's parents when you sit on the empty chair. Discuss some possible questions for the parent, then give the children a few minutes to think of some more questions, in pairs. Ask for a volunteer to be the first person to ask one of the questions, and check that it is suitable. Then sit on the chair to play the role of the parent.

As the parent, you are both surprised and confused. You blame yourself for being too trusting, but feel that Amy may have been just trying to win friends. You have found out that Jo knew about Amy and you are disappointed that Jo didn't tell you. After the children have finished asking questions, come out of role and ask them for their response to the parent.

Then invite some of the children to play the parts of Amy's classmates, so that they can be interviewed by the class. Ask the children who will play the classmates to sit together at the front of the class and give them a few minutes to decide what they know about the situation. While they are doing this, the rest of the class should talk in pairs or groups to think of questions to ask them. Act as the chairperson once the question and answer session starts, but ask questions yourself if necessary.

Now put the class into small groups and ask one child in each group to play the role of Jo. Explain that the others in the group will be Jo's friends, and that the role-play is set after Amy has been found out. During the role-play, Jo must tell her friends that she knew that Amy was taking things but decided to keep quiet. Jo's friends should tell her what they think about this decision. Give the children a minute to think about what they will say before starting the action.

After the role-play, ask the children to help you summarize the arguments that say Jo was right to say nothing and those that say Jo was wrong. Finally, give the children a minute to sit quietly and consider both arguments before voting as the jury. Conclude with a general discussion about when it is right to tell people what you know and when it would be classed as telling tales.

Suggestion(s) for extension

This activity is appropriate for a wide range of abilities, but you would expect a higher level of involvement from more able children. Ask the children who are in role as Amy's friends more searching questions to explore the relationships between Amy and her friends. Ask them questions such as:

▲ Why do you think Amy was taking things?
▲ Is Amy a good friend to you?
▲ Do you give each other presents?
▲ What is the best/worst thing about being friends with Amy?

Try to encourage them to think of the situation from the friends' perspective. You should also demand more interesting dialogue from more confident children during the role-play.

Suggestion(s) for support

After reading the context in section A of the photocopiable sheet to the children, ask them some simple questions to make sure they understand the situation. Children who find it difficult to read the sentences may need a partner to point out where they should put their mark to express their view. Place less confident children with others who will support and include them in the role-play.

Assessment opportunities

Listen in to each role-play situation to assess children's understanding of the issues. Look for children who are able to develop a character when being interviewed as one of Amy's friends. Note any children who ask perceptive questions and those who express themselves clearly both in and out of role.

Performance ideas

Choose a good role-play to develop as a scene for performance. Ask the class to watch and make suggestions on how it might be improved and developed. Add more characters if necessary.

Reference to photocopiable sheet

Photocopiable page 138 provides an imaginary situation for the role-play. It stimulates the children's thinking by requiring them to give their responses to five statements about the imaginary situation.

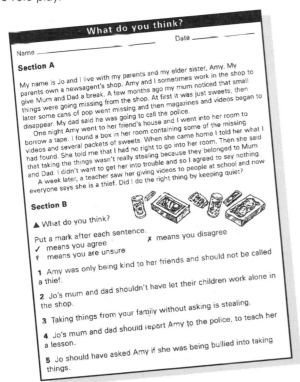

What do you think?

Name _____ Date _____

Section A

My name is Jo and I live with my parents and my elder sister, Amy. My parents own a newsagent's shop. Amy and I sometimes work in the shop to give Mum and Dad a break. A few months ago my mum noticed that small things were going missing from the shop. At first it was just sweets, then later some cans of pop went missing and then magazines and videos began to disappear.

One night Amy went to her friend's house and I went into her room to borrow a tape. I found a box in her room containing some of the missing videos and several packets of sweets. When she came home I told her what I had found. She told me that I had no right to go into her room. Then she said that taking the things wasn't really stealing because they belonged to Mum and Dad. I didn't want to get her into trouble and so I agreed to say nothing.

A week later, a teacher saw her giving videos to people at school and now everyone says she is a thief. Did I do the right thing by keeping quiet?

Section B

▲ What do you think?

Put a mark after each sentence.
✓ means you agree   ✗ means you disagree
? means you are unsure

1 Amy was only being kind to her friends and should not be called a thief.

2 Jo's mum and dad shouldn't have let their children work alone in the shop.

3 Taking things from your family without asking is stealing.

4 Jo's mum and dad should report Amy to the police, to teach her a lesson.

5 Jo should have asked Amy if she was being bullied into taking things.

CENSORING THE MEDIA

To use issues of social debate to stimulate argument in small group improvisations.

†† *Whole class and small groups.*
🕐 *45–60 minutes.*

Previous skills/knowledge needed

Children need to understand what a horror video is and that some cannot be hired or bought by anyone under 18.

Key background information

This activity seeks to develop the skills of argument and

debate in small group improvisations by asking the children to think about the issues from the perspectives of the different characters, before they play the roles. The names and genders of the characters can be changed if necessary.

Preparation
Make one copy per child of photocopiable page 139.

Resources needed
Photocopiable page 139, writing materials.

What to do
Organize the class into small groups, with three in each group. (If a group of four is needed because of class numbers, create another character, such as a friend for Kirsty or another sibling who is about 14 years old.) Give each child a copy of photocopiable page 139 and read it to the class. Talk about some possible arguments that would be appropriate for each character. These could include:

▲ *Craig* – children copy behaviour that they see in violent videos; children do not always understand that horror videos are not real and they may be scared; they can give children nightmares; the children's parents may not approve.

▲ *Kirsty* – Jack is too young to see the horror video and would be scared; I know that it's not real and would not be scared; I am well behaved – only children who already behave badly would copy the violence on the video; I am old enough to make up my own mind about watching horror; horror videos are only a bit of fun, so ten-year-olds should be allowed to watch them.

▲ *Jack* – I know that it's not real and I wouldn't be scared if the others were with me; if I copied what people did on the video I would only pretend to do it; Kirsty is under 18 and she shouldn't be allowed to watch it if I can't; I've seen some frightening things on TV and they didn't give me nightmares.

Give the children a few minutes to write down some of the arguments on their photocopiable sheet. Then ask them to report back on what they have written.

With children sitting in their groups, ask them to use the ideas on their sheet and any other ideas to act out the argument between Craig, Kirsty and Jack. Make it clear that the argument is to involve sensible disagreement only and should not involve physical violence or shouting. They should start at the point when Craig announces that the children will not be allowed to watch the video he has brought. They can use a book to represent the video if necessary. Give the children a few minutes to practise their improvisations. Ask each group to pick out the most interesting part of their improvisation to perform to the class. (With large classes, performances should be limited to a minute.)

Conclude by talking about the issues in the drama and broaden the discussion to talk about censorship of the media in general.

Suggestion(s) for extension
Confident children may like to extend their improvisation to include another scene, showing what happened the next day. Ask them to assume that Jack had watched the horror video and tell them to act out a scene showing what happened when the parents found the video left in the video recorder.

Suggestion(s) for support
Less confident groups can depict a still version of the moment when Craig said no, as if it were part of a comic-strip story. Ask the children to each take on the persona of one of the characters and decide on where they were positioned in the room and what they were feeling at that

moment. Suggest that they think of one thing that the character might be saying, imagining that the text would be written in a speech bubble in the comic strip. Encourage them to use their ideas from the photocopiable sheet to choose an appropriate response for the character.

When they have formed a clear idea of the words their character speaks, tell each child to write the words of their speech bubble on a piece of A4 card. Children can then perform the depictions and speak or read out their characters' speech bubbles.

Assessment opportunities
Look for children who can think of a variety of arguments for each character and then put these into their own words in the improvisation. Note any children who can portray a point of view with conviction during an improvisation.

Performance ideas
Some groups can refine and develop their scenes for performance to a wider audience, or groups can select a small part of their improvisation to script and read onto a tape.

Reference to photocopiable sheet
Photocopiable page 139 provides a context for the improvisation and a writing frame to help children decide on appropriate attitudes and arguments for the characters.

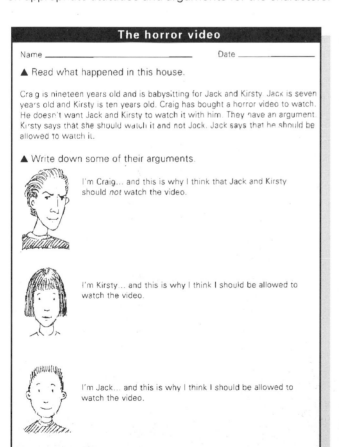

THINKING ABOUT BULLYING

To build children's confidence in using spontaneous improvisation and creating situations for drama.
†† *Whole class, pairs and small groups.*
🕑 *45–60 minutes.*

Previous skills/knowledge needed
Some familiarity with freeze-frames (see 'Significant moments' on page 18) would be helpful but not essential.

Key background information
This activity invites children to invent their own situations to explore and develop through drama and allows them to draw on their own views and experiences to consider the motives and feelings of the characters. The spotlighted conversations develop children's confidence in spontaneous improvisation. The subject matter of the activity also encourages the children to look at the causes and effects of bullying in more depth.

Preparation
Clear an acting area at the front of the class. Make one copy per child of photocopiable page 140.

Resources needed
An acting area, photocopiable page 140, writing materials.

What to do
Put the children into pairs and give one copy of photocopiable page 140 to each child. Read through the sheet to make sure everyone understands it. Give the children a few minutes to talk to their partners about each

Talk about some reasons why the bullying might have happened. Invite the children to explore this further by taking on the roles of pupils at the victim's school. Give pairs of children one minute to think about what they know about the situation as the victim's classmates.

Then ask pairs to make groups of four. Ask the children to imagine that they are sitting in the classroom during registration, talking about the bullying situation but not realizing that the teacher can hear what they are saying. When you say 'Action', the groups should start these conversations. Explain that after a short while, you will play the part of the teacher and walk around the room. When you say 'Freeze', the conversations must stop. You will then stand by a group as a signal that they should restart their conversation so that everyone can hear what they say. When you say 'Freeze', the group should stop. Explain that you will then move to stand by another group who should carry on their conversation in the same way. Explain that these 'spotlighted' conversations represent what the teacher overheard.

Ask the class what they think each character or group of characters feels about what has happened. Include the classmates and the teacher. Now invite the children to decide what course of action the victim should take to stop the bullying. Point out the negative consequences of any inappropriate responses, such as retaliation or revenge, and concentrate on a more acceptable solution, such as telling an adult. Finally, discuss how similar or dissimilar this imaginary incident is compared to real life.

Suggestion(s) for extension
Invite more confident children to be interviewed by the class, as members of the victim's family. Ask them to communicate the effects the bullying is having on the victim's home life.

Suggestion(s) for support
Put less confident children with those who are more confident and will support and include them. Support those who want to take part in the freeze-frame, but are unwilling or unable to speak out a thought, by letting more confident children voice their thoughts for them.

example and then time for each child to write their responses on their own sheet. Make it clear that the sheet is to help them form opinions and that there are no right or wrong answers. When the first pair finish, stop the activity and go through the statements to discuss the responses.

Ask the class to invent an imaginary incident which they all feel would be defined as bullying, such as constant teasing. Invent names for the characters in the situation and make up any other relevant details about the context, such as place, time and how long the bullying has been going on. Emphasize that the characters are entirely fictitious and should bear no resemblance to anyone the children know. Ask a group of children to come into the acting area to make a freeze-frame of the bullying incident. Include witnesses who saw the incident if possible. Now ask various members of the class to make key decisions about where and how the characters should be positioned. Then talk about how each character would be feeling and how this might be conveyed in the freeze-frame. Encourage the children to give reasons for their opinions.

Once the characters' positions and feelings have been determined, ask the class to make suggestions as to what each character might have been thinking at this moment. Try to focus on the attitudes of the characters to what is taking place. Explain that the children in the freeze-frame will be asked to speak out an appropriate thought, as they stand in the depiction. Children playing the characters can choose a thought from the suggestions made by the class or they can think of a suitable thought of their own. Tell the children to make the freeze-frame when you say the word 'Freeze' and then the characters should speak their thoughts in turn.

DRAMA

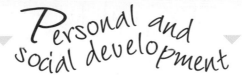

Assessment opportunities

Note those children who are able to make reasonable attempts to define bullying and those who offer appropriate suggestions for the freeze-frame. Use the spotlighting of the conversations to assess children's confidence and imagination when speaking spontaneously in role.

Opportunities for IT

Children could use a word processor to write a few sentences about the bullying as witnessed by the victim's classmates. These could be formatted in a large font so they can be used as part of a class display on the activity.

Performance ideas

Invite groups to rehearse their overheard conversations and then record them onto an audio cassette to play back to the class.

Display ideas

Take a photograph of the freeze-frame, mount it onto a large sheet of sugar paper and position thought bubbles above the heads of the characters. Write text in the bubbles based on appropriate thoughts that emerged in the activity, and glue them in place. Display the sheet alongside a few sentences from each pair which describe the bullying as witnessed by the victim's classmates (see 'Opportunities for IT').

Reference to photocopiable sheet

Photocopiable page 140 provides an introduction to the activity, which helps to stimulate children's thinking when it comes to inventing the situation for the drama.

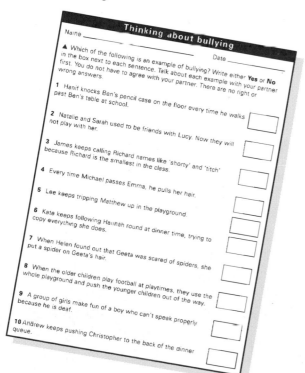

DEAR PROBLEM PAGE

To use an everyday problem as a focus for a variety of drama strategies.

👥 *Whole class and/or pairs.*

🕐 *45–60 minutes.*

Previous skills/knowledge needed

Children should know what a magazine problem page is for and how it works. Some experience of simple drama strategies such as freeze-frames, hot-seating and interviewing in pairs would be an advantage.

Key background information

Children can suggest and/or write their own letters for the problem page. The problem page can then become an ongoing activity, with a different problem tackled every week using one or two different drama strategies each time. Alternatively, you can write a letter yourself to focus on a specific problem or issue that you feel the class will relate to, such as moving to secondary school or sibling rivalry. The strategies covered include freeze-frames, spoken thoughts, hot-seating, paired interviews and role-plays, and forum theatre. Use them all or select those most appropriate for your class. Use the words 'Action' and 'Freeze' to start and stop the drama activities.

Preparation

Write out a letter to the problem page to focus the drama on a particular problem, and make enough copies for the children to share one copy between two. Arrange the chairs in a semicircle.

Resources needed

Copies of the letter (see 'Preparation'), flip chart or board, writing materials, chairs.

What to do

Ask the children to imagine that they work for a children's magazine and that they are responsible for giving advice on the problem page at the back of the magazine. The panel of advisors meets each week to discuss and agree on the advice they will print in response to each letter. Explain that you will play the part of the editor in charge of the advisory panel.

In role as the editor, explain that you have found a good letter for this week's page, but it needs careful thought before writing a reply. Give the children the copies of the letter and ask them to follow it as you read it to them. Talk about their first impressions of the letter and briefly discuss the kind of advice they might give.

Explain that you will now introduce a number of different drama strategies to help them find out more about this problem, before deciding on what advice to give.

▲ *Freeze-frames and spoken thoughts:* make up one or two freeze-frames with spoken thoughts, to illustrate and expand on the events and feelings described in the letter (see 'Significant moments' on page 18). For example, if a letter mentioned sibling rivalry, a freeze-frame could be used to create an example of a situation of this kind. Freeze-frames can be built up gradually after discussion, and characters' thoughts can be based on suggestions made by the whole class. Alternatively, groups can be asked to invent their own freeze-frames and thoughts.

▲ *Hot-seating:* let the class interview some or all of the characters referred to in the letter, using members of the class as the characters.

▲ *Interviews in pairs:* ask pairs to take turns to interview each other, as if they were people associated with the characters in the letter, such as neighbours or school friends. Children should be clear about what questions to ask in paired interviews. They should also be given a time-limit for each interview, to ensure that each child in the pair has the chance to play both roles.

▲ *Paired role-play exercises:* let pairs role-play imaginary situations relating to the problem. For example, if the problem is how to make new friends, pairs can pretend they have never met before and try to start and maintain a conversation for about half to one minute. Some can then be performed to the rest of the class as examples of ways to make new friends.

▲ *Forum theatre:* ask the class to suggest what advice might be appropriate and how it could be carried out. Then invite a small group to enact how one piece of advice could be put into practice, and ask the rest of the class to observe. Explain that observers can ask to stop the action if they want to change anything and the actors can stop the action if they need advice on what to do next. Observers should raise their hand if they want you to stop the action and actors should say the word 'Freeze' if they want to stop. As the situation develops, invite some of the observers to take over the roles. Other pieces of advice can be enacted and developed in the same way with different children as the actors.

▲ *Writing in role:* discuss the main advice that the panel would like to give to the writer of the letter. (Emphasize the importance of negotiation when making decisions as a group.) Then work together with the class to word a suitable letter of reply on the board to communicate the advice.

Suggestion(s) for extension

Ask more confident children to make up short improvisations to illustrate the problem in the letter. Tell them to start and end their scenes with suitable freeze-frames, with spoken thoughts if appropriate.

Suggestion(s) for support

The whole-class discussions will enable you to differentiate questions to support the less confident children. Such children can also be supported by allowing them to work in groups of three or four instead of in pairs.

Assessment opportunities

Note those children who express themselves clearly and confidently in drama, whatever the strategy. Look for children who reveal an understanding of the deeper issues implicit in the problem and note those who communicate these implications through the drama strategies.

Opportunities for IT

The children could use a word processor to write, draft and present their letters, either the original query or the reply to be published in the magazine. They may need to be shown how to use the correct formatting commands to lay out the letter rather than using the space bar to position text. This should include such features as right justification for the address, double spaces between paragraphs, centring for the yours faithfully line and so on.

If the activity is undertaken on a regular basis the reply letters could be published as a magazine, using a desktop publishing package to create the page layout. This might involve the children redrafting the original letters to make them fit the space provided.

Display ideas

Freeze-frames can be sketched to create magazine illustrations for the problem page. These can be displayed alongside the printed magazine version of the letter and the reply (see 'Opportunities for IT').

FRIENDS AND ENEMIES

To extend children's understanding of still image towards a more symbolic dimension.

†† *Whole class, pairs and groups.*

🕐 *45–60 minutes.*

Previous skills/knowledge needed

Children should be confident in using freeze-frames and be able to work co-operatively in pairs and small groups.

Key background information

This activity encourages children to explore ways in which a dramatic image can represent or symbolize an abstract concept, such as friendship or hatred. It then moves on to demonstrate how an abstract image can become the stimulus for a number of realistic improvisations.

Preparation

Clear a large space in the classroom. Make one copy per child of photocopiable page 141.

Resources needed

A large space, photocopiable page 141, writing materials.

What to do

Organize the children into pairs. As a whole class, talk about symbols in everyday life with which the children are familiar, such as pictures on road signs or information signs. Then talk about images that communicate feelings, such as a tear for unhappiness, or communicate events, such as a scythe for New Year. Ask the children to suggest images of their own to portray friendship and hatred. Give one copy of photocopiable page 141 to each child and read it through so that everyone understands what to do. Ask the children

to complete the sheet and share their answers with their partners when they have finished. Differences of opinion should be encouraged in order to stimulate discussion on how and why the images do or do not represent the concepts of friendship and hatred. The image of two faces back to back is deliberately obscure to stimulate speculation and discussion. If children find this image difficult, explain that it could be an image of friendship (as two people joined together) or an image of hatred (as two people turning their backs on each other). Use this to illustrate the subjective nature of some of the more abstract symbols.

Now ask the pairs of children to name themselves A or B. Tell the As to stand in a large circle and the Bs to stand facing their partners just inside the circle. Ask the B children to move back so that they are standing near each other. The B children should now be in an inner circle, facing outwards.

Explain that the inner circle of B children will represent a sculpture entitled 'Friendship'. Each B child will represent a different part of the sculpture. The A child in each pair must tell their partner how to position themselves in the sculpture to represent the idea of friendship. The A children should make the decisions, but the Bs can make suggestions. Talk about some possibilities and encourage the children to think about more symbolic ways to represent friendship using their bodies. Talk about how the body gives messages about the feelings and ask the children to identify the feelings involved in friendship and how these are expressed non-verbally. Give some examples, such as open arms indicating acceptance and comfort or outstretched

hands indicating support. Talk about appropriate expressions using the eyes and mouth and discuss the importance of the position of the head. Discuss the use of different levels and whether high or low levels are significant.

Give the children a time-limit of about half to one minute to complete the task. Then tell the As to stand back, and explain that on a given signal they should walk in a clockwise direction around the sculpture to look at it from all sides. As the A children walk round, point out any similarities or differences in the way friendship has been portrayed. Encourage the Bs to keep as still as possible while they are being observed, but be aware that some children may find their sculpted positions difficult to maintain for any length of time. Ask the B children to try to remember their sculptured positions, as they will be asked to repeat them later on.

Now ask A and B children to swap places, and repeat the activity with the A children being parts of a sculpture entitled 'Hatred'. Discuss some possibilities beforehand if necessary.

Ask the children to sit down as an audience in front of an acting area, and ask one of the A and B pairs to come to the front to make their sculpture poses opposite each other. Ask the class to suggest what might be happening if this were a real-life incident involving the two people. Talk about who, where, when and why it might be happening and what might happen next if you brought the sculptures to life. The pair may need to come out of the freeze every now and again, if the discussion is prolonged. Then let each pair demonstrate their sculptured positions, and invite the class to make suggestions about possible contexts.

Ask the pairs to make their own sculptures into a short improvisation based on a storyline of their own choice. Explain that each improvisation should start with the pair as sculptures who come to life for about one or two

DRAMA

minutes. Make sure the children understand the boundaries of what they are allowed to do in the improvisations (see 'The queue' on page 45). Finally, invite pairs to perform what they have prepared to the class.

Suggestion(s) for extension

Encourage confident children to be more ambitious when directing their partners in the forming of the sculptures. Ask probing questions to help them think about appropriate postures and levels for each sculpture. Suggest that they base their improvisations on the themes of friendship and hatred.

Suggestion(s) for support

Put less confident children in groups of three and let them be a second B in the group.

Assessment opportunities

Look for children who are beginning to think about the themes of friendship and hatred on a more symbolic level. Note those children who have imaginative ideas for turning the paired sculptures into realistic contexts.

Display ideas

Take photographs of the paired sculptures and display them under the title 'Images of friendship and hatred'. Let some children cut out the pictures from their copy of photocopiable page 141, and display them in contrasting pairs under the same title.

Reference to photocopiable sheet

Photocopiable page 141 reveals how images can represent abstract concepts such as friendship and hatred. This acts as an introduction to the sculpturing activity, which uses a different kind of visual image to achieve the same results.

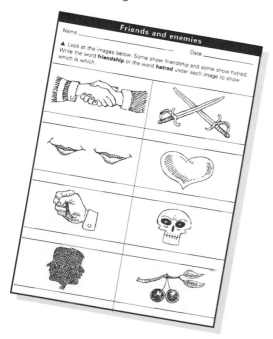

WORLD OF HEALTH AND FITNESS

To give children roles of responsibility within a whole-group drama.

†† *Whole class and small groups.*

🕐 *60 minutes.*

Previous skills/knowledge needed

The children should know what facilities are usually available at a health and fitness centre. They need to be able to work co-operatively in small groups.

Key background information

This activity gives children the power to create and influence the drama. It involves demands being made on the children to deal with problems that come under their remit as workers at the health and fitness centre. The terminology used is intentionally quite formal, for example 'job descriptions', 'team evaluations'. This helps to make the drama feel more realistic.

The activity gives children the opportunity to perform mimes and small group improvisations which lead into and support the whole-group drama within the health and fitness centre.

Preparation

Clear a space in the classroom. Make one copy of photocopiable page 142 per team.

Resources needed

A large space, photocopiable page 142, a large sheet of sugar paper, writing materials.

DRAMA

What to do

Organize the children into teams of three. Ask them to imagine that they all own and work in a newly opened health and fitness centre called World of Health and Fitness. Talk about what such places may offer and then ask them what facilities they would like their own centre to provide. Make a list on the sugar paper.

WORLD OF HEALTH
AND FITNESS

- Weightlifting
- Aerobics
- Swimming
- Yoga
- Indoor rock climbing
- Cycling machines
- Sauna
- Squash
- Ice skating
- Karate

Explain that in the drama you will play the part of the general manager of the centre. Ask the children to play the parts of the workers who work alongside each other in teams to complete a number of jobs. Workers in the same team usually carry out the same jobs. Talk about the kinds of jobs that would need to be carried out before opening to the public and during opening hours. These might include repairing and maintaining equipment, cleaning, making safety checks and preparing healthy food for the health bar. Give one copy of photocopiable page 142 to each team and tell them to look at section A only. Read through section A of the sheet, to make sure everyone understands what to do. Make it clear that section B is for later in the drama.

Tell the children that when they have finished section A of their sheet, they should prepare a short three-part mime sequence to show the class what they do before, during and after opening hours on an ordinary day at work. The whole mime sequence should last no longer than a minute. Encourage the children to improve their mimes by performing the actions a little slower than in real life and ask them to slightly exaggerate the movements. Ask them to include some fine detail in their mimes, such as unzipping tool bags or shaking out dusters before use.

When all the sheets have been completed and most teams have finished their work on the mimes, ask the teams to read out their job descriptions and perform their mimes to the rest of the class.

Now ask the teams to fill in section B of their photocopiable sheets to help them think of some of the advantages and disadvantages of their work. They should then prepare a short improvisation that shows the team talking about their work during a tea break. They should make sure that their conversations include their opinions of their jobs, as written on their sheets. Encourage them to add other things that would make their conversation seem interesting and realistic. These might include references to their home life or where they went last night, or it might include gossip or observations about the customers. Each conversation should last no longer than one to two minutes, during which time all team members should be allowed to speak for a reasonable amount of time. Encourage the children to draft and rehearse their work in small sections, so that they are confident about what to say. Remind them to speak clearly and to speak one at a time, so that the audience is not confused. Talk about putting pauses in the dialogue to vary the pace and add interest. Also make sure that everyone knows what constitutes acceptable behaviour in improvisations.

When most groups have finished, allow the class one final rehearsal and then let the teams perform their conversations to each other. Point out examples of good practice, such as clear diction, interesting dialogue and good use of pace.

Now ask the children to imagine that the workers hold regular staff meetings with the general manager to discuss any problems. Explain that when you say 'Action' the meeting will begin, with yourself in role as the general manager, and the meeting will continue until you say 'Freeze'. In role as the manager, invite the staff to think of solutions to one or more of the following problems:

▲ boisterous behaviour around the pool
▲ litter in the changing rooms and around the centre
▲ customers who do not return small items of equipment
▲ double bookings
▲ a fall in the number of customers overall or at certain times of the day.

Discuss possible solutions to these problems and try to reach a consensus for a successful plan of action before closing the meeting.

Conclude the activity by talking about how closely the drama relates to the real-life problems of a health and fitness centre, and discuss the feasibility of their solutions within a real-life context. Ask the children to talk about how they felt in role as the workers and discuss some of the advantages and disadvantages of this particular kind of job in real life.

Suggestion(s) for extension

Ask more confident children to think about how to make their improvisations more interesting by varying the style. For example, an improvisation could be introduced as a flashback, as if one of the workers were writing an entry in his or her diary:

Tuesday 5 May
My second week at my new job. The tea break was interesting today...

This would then lead into the tea-break conversation.

Mention the use of contrast in making the drama more varied. Make suggestions such as interspersing moments of tension and conflict, in contrast to moments of humour, and inserting moments of dialogue and activity as well as moments of stillness and silence.

Suggestion(s) for support

Put less confident children in teams with children who will include and support them in the mimes and improvisations. Allow cautious children to decide on their level of contribution to the improvisations but encourage them to take part in some capacity, even if it is a non-verbal role. Differentiate through appropriate questioning during the meeting.

Assessment opportunities

Look for children who are able to translate their occupations into concise mime sequences. Note those children who work on their improvisations with a sense of audience, varying the moves and adapting the dialogue to make the work more interesting. Look for children who can express themselves confidently and clearly when giving opinions, and note any children who attempt to maintain their roles as workers at the meeting through characterization and/or a more formal mode of speech.

Opportunities for IT

Some of the solutions to the problems might involve the production of information leaflets. These could be produced using a simple desktop publishing package. Children could explore different styles of leaflet, perhaps using an A4-size format but divided into columns. Alternatively, the children could use an art or drawing package to create suitable posters for display. They may need to be shown how to use clip art or, if a scanner is available, they could be shown how to scan in their own line drawings.

Performance ideas

Some of the more interesting conversations can be adapted to make scripted versions and recorded onto an audio cassette for the class to listen to.

Display ideas

Sketches and information about the health centre and its staff can be collected in the form of a brochure. This can be displayed along with any new posters or leaflets printed on the computer (see 'Opportunities for IT').

Reference to photocopiable sheet

Photocopiable page 142 provides a discussion focus and a writing frame to help the children to make team decisions about their roles as workers in the centre and to help them to form opinions about their work. This prepares them for the improvisations and the meeting to follow.

NOT LIKE US

To use an issue as a focus for developing a whole-group drama experience.

†† *Whole class, pairs and small groups.*

🕐 *Session One: 30 minutes. Session Two: 60 minutes. Session Three: 60 minutes. Session Four: 60 minutes.*

Previous skills/knowledge needed

The children should know how volcanic eruptions have affected the inhabitants of volcanic islands in the past. Familiarity with freeze-frames would be helpful.

Key background information

This activity is divided into four sessions to be spread over a number of weeks. Session One can take place in the classroom but Sessions Two to Four require a larger space. The first two sessions involve building a sense of

identification with an island community. This helps the children to feel the impact of the prejudice against them in the last two sessions. The drama seeks to help children understand the effects of prejudice from the point of view of the victims and works to stimulate discussion on the issue. Whole-group drama, small group improvisations and ritual are among the drama strategies employed to build belief and develop the children's commitment to their role within an imaginary community. This helps the children perform their roles with sincerity and integrity and helps to improve the overall quality of the drama experience.

Preparation

Sessions One and Two: make one copy per child of photocopiable page 143. Session Three: make one copy of photocopiable page 144. Session Four: make one copy of photocopiable page 145 and place it in an envelope. Write

the following kinds of graffiti across sheets of sugar paper, using scribbled writing and thick black and red felt-tipped pens: *Volcano Islanders go home. Volcano Islanders cause trouble. Volcano ceremonies are evil. Volcano people are bad. Keep Shern free of Volcanoes. Volcano people are not like us. Be warned!*

Resources needed

Session One: photocopiable page 143, flip chart or board, paper, writing materials. Session Two: a large space, photocopiable page 143, children's job descriptions from Session One. Session Three: a large space, photocopiable page 144, clipboard. Session Four: a large space, sugar paper, photocopiable page 145, envelope, writing materials.

What to do
Session One

Give each child a copy of the map of Volcano Island on photocopiable page 143 and explain that the next series of drama lessons will be about something that happened to the people who lived on this imaginary island. Tell the children that they will be invited to play the parts of the island people during these lessons. Talk about the details on the map and what kind of place it represents.

Divide the class into four large groups and number the groups one to four. Explain that these numbers correspond to four of the squares on the map and indicate the area in which they live. Tell each child to select and shade in a row of houses within their allocated square on the map to indicate more precisely where they live on the island. Children can decide to live in the same row of houses if they wish.

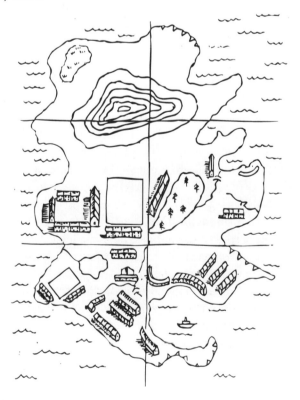

Ask the children to play the parts of the adults who work on the island. Discuss some possible occupations and write these on the board for reference. Then ask the children to invent the name, age and occupation of the character they will play in the drama and to write it down on a sheet of paper. What would they do on a typical working day? Ask them to jot down a few ideas to form a brief job description.

Explain that the drama will start on an ordinary day when the people are ready to start work. Ask the children to underline the job they will do first in the drama (put the children into pairs to help each other with this task; pairs can decide to share the same job if they wish). Collect in the maps and writing for use in Session Two.

Session Two

Ask the children to sit at one end of the room, in their pairs. Give out the maps and the job descriptions from Session One and ask the children to look at these to remind themselves of the island and their roles. Explain that they will need to mime the jobs in the drama. Give the pairs a few minutes to decide on how best to mime their particular jobs. Now ask them to imagine that the room represents the four parts of the island indicated by the squares on the map. Make sure they know which part of the room represents their square. Then define any areas of the room that are out of bounds for the drama.

Ask the children to talk to their partners to decide roughly where they will need to be positioned to start their first job of the day. Then collect in the maps and job descriptions. Make sure the children understand that while they are miming the actions during the drama they will be allowed to speak to each other in role.

Tell them that the drama will begin with a 'frozen' moment, as they start their first jobs. The island will come

to life when you say 'Action' and stop when you say 'Freeze'. Give the children a few minutes to decide how their bodies will be positioned in the 'frozen' moment and tell them to fold their arms when they have decided. Now gradually build up the initial freeze by asking a few pairs at a time to take up their 'frozen' positions on the island.

When everyone is in position, say 'Action' to start the drama. Let the drama carry on for several minutes and then call 'Freeze' to stop the action.

Gather the children to one side of the room and then let the four numbered groups take turns to perform some of the things they were doing during the drama. Keep these performances short and invite the audience to comment on the things they liked about each group's performance. Comment on any examples of detailed and accurate mime and interesting dialogue.

Tell the children that every year the islanders hold a short but special ceremony to remember those who lost everything they owned many years ago when the volcano erupted. The island was covered with ash after everyone had been evacuated. The ceremony is held in the meeting hall on the island. Ask the children to help you make up a suitable ritual that can be performed by everyone in a circle. This might include stylized actions to represent the eruption of the volcano and the covering of the island with ash. It may also include chants or a narration to relate the people's feelings at having to leave their homes and returning to find them destroyed. Use the children's ideas as much as possible but keep the actual ceremony short and simple. Encourage the children to justify their suggestions in terms of appropriate symbolism.

Explain that for this part of the drama you will take on the role of the islander who directs the ceremony each year. Practise the ceremony a few times and then perform it in role. Stay in role as the director of the ceremony and announce that you have some bad news. Stop the drama and tell the children that they will continue the story in the next drama lesson. The fact that the children do not know what the bad news is will act as a cliffhanger and will encourage group discussion and speculation in the intervening period leading up to the next lesson. This makes use of tension to keep children committed and interested in the drama, as the story unfolds.

Session Three

Tell the children that you will start the drama where it finished at the end of the last lesson. Take on the role of the director of the ceremony and tell the islanders that the scientists who monitor the volcano have sent an urgent message that there will be an eruption in the next few weeks. Explain that you kept the news from them because you didn't want to spoil the ceremony. Tell the islanders that arrangements will be made for an evacuation when you know which country will be your host. Suggest that the islanders walk to their favourite part of the island and sit down in silence to think about what they will miss most about the island. Let the islanders do this, and then stop the drama and ask a few children to share their thoughts about leaving.

Now ask the children to imagine that two days later, the islanders received a letter from a nearby island called Shern, inviting them to stay there. Read out the letter printed on photocopiable page 144 and ask the children for their reactions. Make it clear that the island is in such danger that the islanders have no choice but to accept the invitation made by Shern. Explain that if the eruption is as bad as predicted, the islanders may never return. Restart the drama

on the night before the evacuation and tell the islanders to go home and pack something small to remind them of their life on the island. When most children have finished packing, stop the drama and call the children together.

Ask the children to imagine that time has moved on, to the moment when they arrive at Shern to be met by one of the officials, as promised in the letter. Tell the children that when they arrived, there was no one there and so they waited. After an hour, an official arrived with a clipboard. Tell the children that when you pick up the clipboard, you will play the part of the official from Shern and when you put it down you will come out of role. In role as the official, be pleasant but very officious. Do not encourage the islanders to ask any questions or attempt to engage them in any dialogue. Apologize for your lateness and explain that you have been arranging accommodation for the islanders. Tell the islanders that the promised hotel is not ready and that you have arranged temporary accommodation for them in a nearby boathouse.

Lead the way across the hall to the imaginary boathouse and give the islanders a conducted tour of the facilities. They must sleep on straw mattresses and have one box by each mattress for their things. The weather is warm enough to do without any heating but they will need to place a bucket under the holes in the roof if it rains. The

toilets are outside and there are cold showers only. The Sherns have managed to install a few camping stoves and have supplied them with plenty of gas containers for all their cooking needs. Explain that the nearest shops are half a mile away in the town. If the islanders protest, keep insisting that this is only a temporary arrangement and then leave them to unpack their things. Put down the clipboard and stop the drama.

Tell the children that, after the official had gone, the islanders unpacked their things and talked to each other about what had happened. Explain that they should now mime the unpacking and talk to each other about how they feel as they unpack. Stop the drama after a few minutes and tell the children that the story will continue in the next drama lesson.

Session Four

Tell the children that the day after the islanders arrived in Shern, they received another visit from the official. Pick up the clipboard to start the drama. In role as the official, apologize for any inconvenience and promise that the hotel will be ready soon. Explain that the work they hoped to offer them is now unavailable and so they will have to work in a factory instead. Their first week's wage will be taken to pay for the cost of the camping stoves. If the islanders object, then suggest that they take their complaints to the town hall. Stop the drama and ask the children how they feel about the situation.

Ask the children to imagine that the islanders went to the town hall every day for the next seven days to complain, but when they arrived it was always closed. They also noticed that when they went into the shops, the shopkeepers would always serve the Shern people first and when they tried to make conversation with the Sherns, they were ignored. When they walked down the streets, Sherns crossed over the road to avoid meeting them. Put the children into small groups and ask them to make up a short improvisation to show how they were treated by the Sherns when they went to town. Make it clear that some of the group will need to play the parts of Sherns. Give the children a few minutes to work on their improvisations and then when they are ready, they should perform them to each other.

Ask the children to sit in a semicircle and talk about why the Sherns might be behaving in this way. Suggest that the islanders might perform their special ceremony to make them feel more at home. Start the drama again and re-create the ceremony, as if you were the director as before. Stop the drama and tell the children to sit down in the circle.

Explain that on the morning after the islanders held their ceremony, they heard that the volcano had erupted and destroyed all their homes. On that same morning, something else happened. They found some papers pinned to their doors and walls. Spread out the graffiti on the floor for the children to read and ask them what they feel. Introduce the word 'prejudice' if the children have not already used it and talk, out of role, about what the islanders could do. Explain that returning to Volcano Island is not an option at the moment as it is too dangerous. Allow genuine angry responses and acknowledge feelings of revenge and hatred, but try to focus on what they could do to improve relations with the Sherns.

In the middle of the discussion tell the children that while the islanders were talking, someone came and put an envelope under the door of the boathouse and then ran away. Bring out a copy of the letter on photocopiable page 145 and read it to the children. Discuss whether or not they should accept the invitation and why. Ask each child to make up their own mind as to whether they would go to the party if they were an islander, and ask them to vote.

Finally, use the events that have taken place in the drama and the feelings these have aroused to open up a discussion on prejudice.

DRAMA

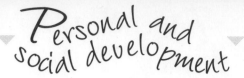
Suggestion(s) for extension

Session One: encourage the children to write about their roles in more detail. Session Two: let more confident children perform their jobs to the class in small groups or pairs, rather than as part of a larger group and encourage them to use more dialogue. Session Three: ask more confident children to tell the class how they feel about leaving the island and encourage them to talk about the implications if they are not able to return. Session Four: encourage the children to think about appropriate expressions and the use of silence to create tension in their improvised scenes.

Suggestion(s) for support

Put less confident children in pairs or mixed-ability groups for the writing and for the various drama activities. Differentiate through questioning when discussing things in a whole group.

Assessment opportunities

Session One: look for children who can write in role with ease. Session Two: note those children who take on their roles with integrity, using appropriate dialogue and characterization. Look for children who can empathize with the islanders having to leave their island. Session Three: note those children who respond to the reception in Shern with appropriate dialogue and feeling, when they unpack as the islanders in the boathouse. Session Four: look for children who can devise and perform suitable improvisations, which indicate the level of prejudice being experienced.

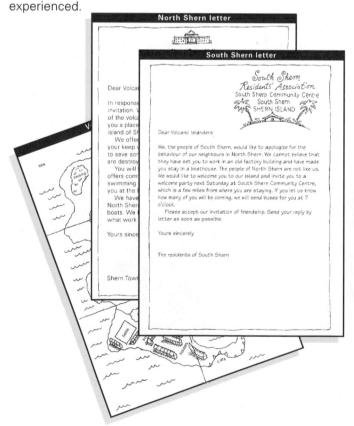

Opportunities for IT

The children could use an encyclopaedia or newspaper CD-ROMs to search for information on volcanic eruptions and their effects. If the school has access to the Internet, the children could also search for up-to-date information about current volcanic eruptions.

The children could create their own volcano magazine or newspaper using a word processor or desktop publishing package. They could write about their own role-play experiences as if they were reporting the events as they took place. The accounts could be written from contrasting viewpoints and in different genres.

Performance ideas

The ceremony can be developed to include music, poetry reading and other activities, against a backdrop of pictures and posters of volcanoes, to be performed to a wider audience. Some children may like to make up an improvisation about what happened when some of the islanders met the Sherns at the welcome party.

Display ideas

Children can colour in the part of the island where they live on the map and these can be displayed, together with the job descriptions they have written. Some children may like to write diary entries to express their feelings about leaving Volcano Island and arriving in Shern.

Reference to photocopiable sheets

Photocopiable page 143 provides a visual focus for the drama, which helps children to identify with the island and its inhabitants. Photocopiable page 144 provides a letter of invitation, which is used as a symbol of hope. The existence of this letter makes the impact of the prejudice even more acute, when the islanders realize that they have been betrayed. Photocopiable page 145 provides another letter, which represents a gesture of friendship, even if the children choose to reject it. This provides a balance in terms of how people view outsiders.

CIRCUS

To use a topical issue as a focus for developing whole-group drama.

✝✝ *Whole class and small groups.*

⏲ *Session One: 15–20 minutes. Session Two: 45–60 minutes.*

Previous skills/knowledge needed

Children should be familiar with traditional circus activities and should understand basic circus terminology such as 'big top', 'trapeze artist' and so on, as well as being familiar with freeze-frames (see 'Significant moments' on page 18).

Key background information

This activity seeks to open up a debate on whether animals should be used in a circus; the children are put into the role of circus employees who have to make a decision on this. The drama works to build up a commitment to the circus, so the children feel motivated to enter into the debate. It gives children an opportunity to take on unusual roles and engage in challenging mime work, as they attempt to play the parts of circus workers. Use the words 'Action' and 'Freeze' to start and stop the drama each time.

Preparation

Session One: make one copy per child of photocopiable page 146. Session Two: make one copy of photocopiable page 147 and cut out your chosen letter.

Resources needed

Session One: photocopiable page 146, flip chart or board, writing materials. Session Two: a large space, photocopiable page 147, scissors.

What to do

Session One

Explain that in this drama lesson you will be asking the children to play the parts of people who have applied for a job at a newly formed circus called Brown's Circus. Put the children into pairs and ask them to answer one copy each of photocopiable page 146, thinking about whether each item would be relevant at a circus and drawing a line to the box that they think is the most appropriate for each. Explain that the completed sheets will enable the class to find out what the general public will expect the circus to offer. Read through the sheet, ensuring that the children understand that they are to indicate what they think will be the public's expectations, not their own. Allow the children to talk with their partners to help them if they wish.

After completion, go through the list on the sheet and ask the children to raise their hands to indicate how they answered – how many put 'Yes' to 'Lions and/or tigers', how many put 'Maybe' and how many put 'No'. Record the results on the board and identify about ten of the most popular activities.

Ask the children to imagine that this list was sent to Mr and Mrs Brown, the owners of the circus, who decided that all the items on the list should be included in their first show.

Tell the children that the first circus show is to be performed in a field at the edge of a large town. Explain that the drama will start after the workers have parked their vehicles in the field. The action will start with the workers setting up for their performances. Refer to the list of acts and talk about what this preparation would involve. Then ask each child to decide what their job will be at the circus and what they will need to do at the start of the drama. Some children may not be performers, as they will have other responsibilities such as looking after animals or fixing equipment. Give the children a few minutes to discuss their choice with their partner and to write it down in note form on the back of the photocopiable sheet. Read out the list of activities to be offered at the circus and ask the children to indicate which ones are related to their chosen job. Group the children according to similar occupations as far as possible in preparation for Session Two.

Session Two

Sit the children together but in their groups. Ask them to imagine that the classroom represents the field and that their circus vehicles are parked around the edge. Define any areas of the room that are out of bounds for the drama. Explain that all the actions must be mimed, but the children should speak to each other in the drama, as if they really were the circus workers.

Tell the children that the drama will start with the workers unloading their vehicles and then continue with the workers carrying out their jobs. Assign an area of the room to each group for their imaginary vehicles and tell them to sit in their allocated areas. Make some suggestions for appropriate mimes if necessary before the children begin.

Let the drama carry on for several minutes or until a few children begin to lose concentration. Then stop the action and call the class together. Invite the children (a few groups at a time) to perform to the class some of the things they have been doing. Keep each performance short and use it as an opportunity to point out examples of good mime and interesting dialogue.

Now ask the class to imagine that the circus owners wanted some photographs to advertise the circus in a magazine article. Give the children a few minutes to work in groups to make a freeze-frame to represent a photograph that would reflect their jobs. Ask them to think of a caption for their photograph. Then let each group show their freeze-frame to the class.

Tell the children that on the day before the first performance, the workers were called to an emergency meeting by one of the owners. Explain that at the meeting you will play the part of Mr (or Mrs) Brown. Start the drama at the meeting. In role as Mr Brown, tell the workers that you have received a letter, and read out the most appropriate letter from a copy of photocopiable page 147. Explain that if this is not sorted out, the council may withdraw their permission for the circus to use the field and there could be some bad publicity. When you have finished reading the letter, ask the class for their response. Explain that you will be writing a reply and want to know how the workers think you should respond. Stress the need to make reasonable arguments to avoid bad publicity.

Stop the drama, and use this as an opportunity to reflect on the real-life arguments for and against using animals in the circus. After the discussion, tell the children to stand facing you in a large semicircle. Explain that you will make a few statements that represent different points of view about this issue. After each one has been spoken, the children should move according to their opinions in the following manner: if they strongly agree they should walk towards you and sit as near to you as possible without touching you or anyone else; if they strongly disagree, they should remain standing where they are; if their opinions are somewhere in between, they should stand between those who are sitting and those who are standing.

As children make their opinions known, ask one or two why they chose to position themselves in the way they did. They may offer statements similar to the following:
▲ I think that using animals in a circus is cruel.
▲ I think that it's OK to use animals in a circus, as long as they are treated well.
▲ I think that using animals in circuses should be banned.
▲ I think that circuses can help save wild animals from extinction.

Now tell the children that the Browns decided that they didn't want to start a circus with all these problems and so the workers found jobs in other circuses of their own choice.

children and adults. These could be recorded in a simple database so that the results can be analysed by the children and presented graphically.

Children could also use a word processor to write, draft and present a letter from the Browns to the council about the circus. The children may need to be shown how to use the correct formatting commands to lay out the letter, such as double spacing or indents for new paragraphs.

Performance ideas

Ask some groups to make up a short mime sequence showing a circus act without animals, and ask other groups to make up one showing an act that does use animals. These can then be performed to music.

Reference to photocopiable sheets

Photocopiable page 146 is used to focus the children's minds on the activities in a conventional circus and seeks to encourage them to think about opinions other than their own. Photocopiable page 147 provides three options for a letter of complaint, stimulating discussion on the issue of using animals in a circus. Your choice of letter will depend upon what the circus in the drama already includes in terms of animals.

Suggestion(s) for extension

Expect more detailed answers and responses from more confident children during the discussions, in and out of role. After the agreed list is made at the end of Session One, ask the children to make a tape recording to represent a short radio advert for their circus.

Suggestion(s) for support

Put less confident children in pairs with more able children for all the activities and ask each pair to share the same job during Session Two. Differentiate through questioning during the discussions in and out of role.

Assessment opportunities

Look for children who are unable to make the distinction between their own views and that of the general public when filling in the photocopiable sheet in Session One. Note children who use accurate and imaginative mime to carry out their jobs in Session Two and note those who add appropriate dialogue. Look for children who are fairly confident in a group role-play, but less confident when performing to the whole class.

Opportunities for IT

After Session One of the activity, some children could use an art package to create a flyer advertising the different attractions of the circus.

Children could also create a questionnaire about circus animals and collect a wider sample of replies from other

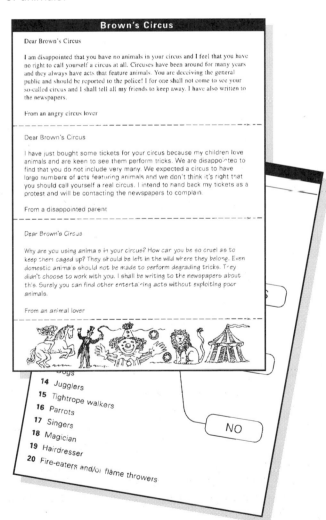

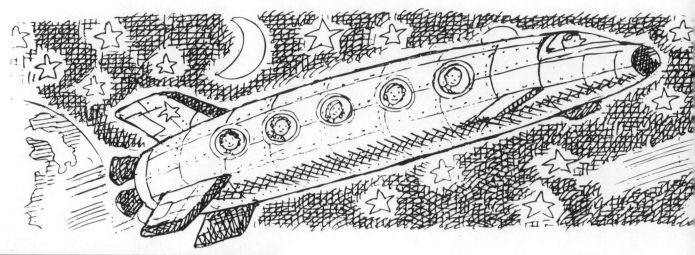

NEW SETTLERS

To develop children's confidence in solving problems and negotiating decisions in role.

†† *Whole class, pairs and small groups.*

🕐 *60 minutes.*

Previous skills/knowledge needed

Children need to understand what the term 'air pollution' means and need to be aware of some of the effects this can have on people's health.

Key background information

This activity invites children to solve problems and make decisions in role as characters within a drama. By encouraging children to develop a sense of community within a dramatic context, they become motivated to negotiate their own community rules. This develops children's skills and confidence in speaking in role within the large class group, as well as in smaller groups. Some classes may be ready to hold the community discussion without the intervention of a teacher, but others may need you to act as chairperson. It may be worth letting classes start on their own, and then you can be prepared to step in if necessary. Use the words 'Action' and 'Freeze' to start and stop the drama each time.

Preparation

Make one copy of photocopiable page 148 per pair of children.

Resources needed

A large space, photocopiable page 148, a set of things that can be worn by all the class (such as PE bands or sticky labels on jumpers), a large sheet of paper, writing materials.

What to do

Tell the children that they are going to be invited to take part in a drama set in the future. Explain the following context for the drama.

The earth's air has become so polluted that large groups of people are settling on other newly discovered planets that have been found to have conditions similar to our own. The new settlers travel in small, specially designed spaceships that enable them to take only essential provisions to keep them going until they become self-sufficient. The people undergo training in self-sufficiency skills such as farming, building, sewing and cooking before they go.

Ask the children to play the parts of new settlers who attempt to set up a new life on another planet similar to Earth but less heavily populated. Talk about what skills they would need in order to be self-sufficient. Organize the children into pairs. Then give out one copy of photocopiable page 148 to each pair and ask them to decide on what they will pack. As pairs complete their sheets, they should then begin to move into the room to mime packing their chosen things for the journey and pretend to put them in a given central area.

Gather the children together and ask them to put on the items to identify them as new settlers (for example, the PE bands). Explain that sometimes you will play the part of one of their group by wearing one of these items. Make it clear that when you are not wearing the item, you will not be in the drama.

Tell the children that a meeting was called to check on the equipment and provisions. Ask pairs to bring their sheets to refer to and then sit with the children in a circle or semicircle. Put on your item of identification and start the meeting by reading through the list on the sheet and asking who has decided to take what. Then ask the settlers to decide if they want to take any weapons and why. If the group cannot agree, then leave it to individuals to make up their own minds. Stop the drama.

Explain that you are now going to move time on, to the first day on the new planet. Talk about the initial jobs that would need to be done. Put pairs together to form groups and allocate an area where each group will live. Tell each group to sit in their area and share out the jobs for the day.

consider the negative consequences of any suggestions involving fighting.

Ask the settlers to talk about what laws they would want, while you check that the settlement is safe from the lawless neighbours. Then leave the group and wait to see what happens. If the children find it difficult to talk without you being there, return to direct the discussion. If the children begin to talk in small groups, return after a short while and invite groups to share their ideas. If the class are able to talk as a whole group, leave them as long as possible before returning to ask what has been discussed in your absence.

Now take a large sheet of paper and write down what the settlers feel to be the most important laws. Stop the drama and tell the children that when the laws were eventually passed on the planet, the whole planet became a safer place to live.

Talk about the laws the children know of in this country and discuss why it is important to have laws. Talk about laws in the past that now seem harsh, such as the ban on feeding beggars in Tudor times. Talk about how changes in society can create a desire for new laws, such as privacy laws to protect famous people from the press.

Suggestion(s) for extension

Encourage the children to give clear reasons for their opinions during the discussions. Ask them to think about the implications of making laws, in terms of enforcement and punishment. Demand more detailed dialogue in the improvised conversations.

Suggestion(s) for support

Put less confident children into mixed-ability pairs and groups for all the activities. Differentiate through questioning in discussion and join in to support those who need help during the whole-group mimed activities.

Give the children a time-limit and ask them to fold their arms when they have completed the task. Define which areas of the room are to be used in the drama and make it clear that they will need to mime the actions but not the talking – that is, they can talk out loud. Then start the drama by sending groups out to start their jobs. Watch the drama from the side of the room, but join in if you feel that the children need support. Let this carry on for several minutes.

Stop the drama and restart it again at a meeting in which you invite the settlers to report back on what they have accomplished during the first day. Ask them how they all feel at this point and whether they can foresee any problems. Discuss anything which arises and then tell them that another group of settlers will be arriving shortly to live on the adjoining land. Talk about the implications of this and ask the settlers to decide whether they want to put up some barriers to define their part of the planet.

Stop the drama and move time on – it is now a month later, when the settlers are comparing their new lives with the ones back on Earth. Talk about what they might miss and what they would enjoy about their new lives. Then ask the children to work in their groups to prepare a short improvisation. This should consist of a brief conversation between the settlers to reveal how each of them now feels about living on the new planet. Then let groups perform their improvisations to the class.

Sit the children in a circle and start the whole-group drama again, as if you were chairing a meeting. Tell the settlers that you have received a message from some of their new neighbours, who have just arrived on the planet. A few of the new neighbours are fighting over the best pieces of land. Some have brought weapons and are using them against each other. Many of the new neighbours are frightened and want the existing settlers to help them make some laws for the whole planet in order to keep the peace. They have promised to be in touch again in about a week.

Talk about the possible effects of having no laws on the planet. Issues of defence may arise and some children may wish to discuss weapons again. Let the children express their opinions and explore options but make sure they

DRAMA

Assessment opportunities

Look for children who use imaginative mime and appropriate dialogue in the role-play activities. Note those children who are able to appreciate the implications of having no laws on the new planet and those who are able to give reasons for their opinions during the discussions.

Opportunities for IT

The children could use a word processor to draft and present the laws for their settlement. They could also search for other laws, from different CD-ROMs, the Internet or reference books so that these can be presented in a class wall display. The children could also experiment with different-sized formats, for example a credit-card-sized set of rules that the settlers can carry with them. Children will need to be shown how to reformat their text to make the rules fit the different-sized formats.

Display ideas

Children can rewrite the new laws to indicate their importance, using special paper and appropriate handwriting and phraseology. This can then be displayed along with other examples of community laws, such as the ten commandments.

Reference to photocopiable sheet

Photocopiable page 148 provides a list of equipment that the imaginary settlers might need to start life on a new planet. This helps the children to decide what to pack, giving them more time to spend on miming the packing. The things on the list also indicate the kind of lifestyle that the settlers can expect on the new planet, which prepares the children for the drama to come.

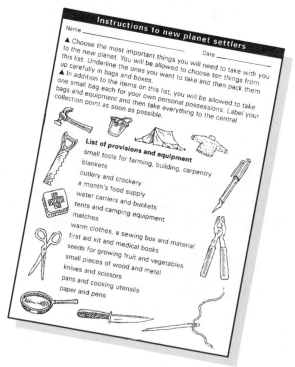

DRAMA GAMES

To use drama games to develop social skills to support ongoing work in drama.

†† *Whole class and pairs.*

🕐 *10–20 minutes per activity.*

Key background information

Some of these activities are designed to help new groups learn each other's names and begin to bond together as a group. Others are designed to develop existing relationships within the group. All the activities require some degree of co-operation between group members, which helps to improve the social health of the group. These games and exercises are best used as activities in their own right rather than as warm-up sessions for drama lessons. Choose the games that are most appropriate for the needs of your class. Use the whistle to stop the activities when children would find it difficult to hear your voice.

Preparation

Arrange the children's chairs in a large circle. All games require the children to be in pairs.

Resources needed

A large space with enough chairs for all the children, a whistle.

What to do

Game 1: Tell me one thing about yourself

Ask the children to sit in a circle on the chairs, next to their partners. Ask each child to think of a short sentence that will reveal something about themselves. They should choose a piece of information that they are prepared to share with the group. The sentence should start with the words 'My name is…' and should then continue with more information. Give some examples such as:

▲ My name is Russell and I play football every night with my younger brother.

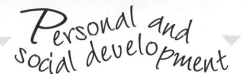

▲ My name is Lai Ching and my sister annoys me when she plays loud music in her room.

Encourage the children to choose something they can easily remember. Allow a few minutes for them to prepare a sentence each, with partners helping each other.

When everyone has a sentence prepared, tell the class to stand up inside the circle of chairs and then go around as many people as they can, to tell them their sentence and listen to what everyone else has to say. Warn them that after a few minutes, they will be asked to try to remember what other people said. Say 'Go' to start the activity and stop the action after a few minutes. Ask everyone to sit in the circle. Then point to one of the children and ask the class to tell you this child's name and sentence. Repeat this until every child has been selected.

Game 2: Acting a favourite pastime

Stand the children in a circle. Ask each child to think of one of their favourite pastimes and then make up an action to represent it. For example, playing football might involve a kicking action, and looking after pets might involve a stroking action. Give a few more examples and then let the children talk in pairs to help each other make up their actions.

When they are ready, explain the activity in the following way: one child steps into the circle and says her own name. She should perform her action as she says her name. Then everyone else should step into the circle, repeat this child's name and copy her action. Everyone then moves back to the edge of the circle, including the first child. This sequence is then repeated with the next child stepping into the circle, until everyone has had a turn.

Game 3: Keep your prisoner

Ask one child in each pair to sit on the chairs in the circle. Then ask their partners to stand behind them. You need one empty chair with a child standing behind it for this game. If you have an even number of children, then arrange for one child sitting down to stand out for a few minutes, on a rota basis. The child standing out can be the referee, in case of any disagreements.

Explain that in this game the children standing up are guarding their prisoners. Point out that the guard standing behind the empty chair has no prisoner. Guards can obtain a new prisoner by calling out the name of someone else's prisoner. When a prisoner hears her name, she must move to sit in the chair of the guard who has called her. However, guards can prevent their prisoners from leaving by touching them on the shoulders before they get the chance to move on. Guards are not allowed to move away from their posts to do this and so they must act quickly as soon as they hear their prisoner's name being called by another guard.

Any guard guilty of mistreating their prisoner by hitting instead of touching will lose their prisoner. Guards are only allowed to touch prisoners on the shoulder, not on the back or head. Whichever guard has no prisoner must keep calling different names until they obtain one.

Remember to keep changing the referee, and change guards and prisoners around regularly to give all the children a chance to try both parts.

Game 4: Follow the hand

Ask pairs to name themselves A and B. Ask child B to imagine that her nose is fixed to the centre of child A's hand by a length of invisible elastic. Child A should slowly move one of her hands in different directions, with palms facing outwards. Child B should try to follow wherever A's hand moves, keeping her nose near child A's palm. Explain that A has the power to take B where she likes, but they will soon swap over these roles and so it will be in A's interest to be kind to B!

After a few minutes, stop the action and tell the children to swap roles. Encourage the children to co-operate to make the activity work and suggest that they use slow movements to make it work well. After both partners have had a turn, ask children whether they preferred to be the leader or the follower and why.

Game 5: Spot the leader

Ask the children to sit in the circle on the chairs, and then ask one pair of children to come out of the circle and turn their backs, so they are unable to see the group. Point silently to one child in the circle who will be the leader.

The pair are now asked to return and must try to guess who the leader is. The children in the circle must copy everything the leader does. Explain that the leader can do any action she likes, as long as it is not rude or silly. Actions might include tapping feet, scratching the head, standing on one leg or rubbing the hands. The leader can remain sitting or stand up to move, but she should not move away from the area in front of her chair. The leader must change her actions every time you blow the whistle, which should be approximately every ten seconds. This should carry on for about a minute. The pair on the outside of the group should watch all the actions before trying to guess who the leader is. They can be given three guesses. Repeat this with a different pair each time.

Suggestion(s) for extension

Game 1: encourage the children to make up longer and/or more complex sentences. Game 2: encourage the children to make up more detailed mimes for their actions in the circle. Game 3: make the activity more challenging by asking guards to call out the initials of the prisoners instead of the names. If two prisoners have the same initials they should each be given a different number to add to their initials. Game 4: ask the children to speculate as to why some people may prefer to be a follower rather than a leader and encourage them to think of real-life examples of roles of power with responsibility. Game 5: give more confident leaders less time for each activity to encourage a greater range of actions. Let more confident children guess the leader as individuals instead of as a pair.

Suggestion(s) for support

Game 1: pair up less able children with those who are more confident. Offer help to those who need support to make up a sentence. Let the children stay with their partners when sharing their sentences with the others. Game 2: children with low self-esteem may find it overwhelming to step into the circle to say their name and perform their action and may be happier carrying out the action without stepping into the circle. For some children, you could offer to say the child's name yourself while you both perform the action. Alternatively, ask the child to show you her action, and then step into the circle on the child's behalf to say her name and perform her action. Game 3: if some children are being overlooked by the guards and not being chosen as prisoners, restrict the choice of prisoners to those who have never escaped – that is, those who have not been called. Games 4 and 5: put less confident children in pairs with children who will support them. In game 5, let less confident children who are to be leaders practise three or four actions with the class, before the pair return to watch and guess.

Assessment opportunities

Look for children who co-operate with others to make the games work. Note those who take the lead with confidence when invited to do so.

Opportunities for IT

The children could extend the work carried out in the activity by using a word processor to write and present the rules for the different drama games. These could be presented as a large printout which can be used to remind children of the rules of the games, or they could be compiled into a class book of drama games.

Display ideas

Ask the children to write out the sentence they made up in Game 1, but ask them to omit their names. Put these on display under a 'Guess who?' title, along with a full list of the children's names.

DRAMA

Cross-curricular themes

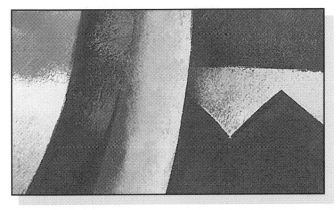

Drama strategies are also good teaching strategies and as such they can be applied to aspects of most subjects with success. They offer an active and imaginative approach, which can easily be included in the planning of most subjects, to support children's knowledge and understanding across the curriculum.

In this chapter children are given the opportunity to learn about history from the perspective of imaginary participants such as villagers, soldiers and archaeologists. From these roles they are confronted with some of the dilemmas and problems faced by the people of the time and asked to come up with their own solutions. This helps children identify with times which can often seem remote and obscure. Working in role can also provide a motivation for historical research, as children strive to make their dramatic representations of the past as accurate as possible.

Drama can also be usefully employed to explore aspects of geography. Imaginary contexts can be used as a framework for real-life issues involving land use and the community. Some of the activities in this chapter are based around imaginary locations such as a village and a campsite and deal with topical issues such as the conflicting interests of residents and developers.

This chapter includes an activity relating to the use of physical theatre to represent numbers in maths work. This activity involves children in computation work in an active way. Movement is also included in another drama activity, where actions are preceded by sounds to introduce a factory environment.

HISTORICAL VILLAGE

To build confidence in playing roles within a whole-group historical context.

†† *Whole class and groups.*

⏱ *Session One: 45 minutes. Session Two: 45 minutes. Session Three: 45 minutes.*

Previous skills/knowledge needed

The children should have some background knowledge about everyday life in the chosen historical period.

Key background information

This activity is intended to form part of ongoing work on a historical period and can be adapted to suit the problems and experiences that are appropriate to that period. Small items of costume can be worn during Session Two, but this is not essential and should be kept to a minimum. Sessions One and Three are designed to take place in a classroom, but Session Two needs a hall or similar large space. Use the words 'Action' and 'Freeze' to start and stop the drama each time.

Preparation

Session One: ensure that the children have access to information about six common village occupations of the period, for example blacksmiths, grocers, fishermen, farmers, carpenters, builders if you are focusing on the Victorian period. Make one copy per child of photocopiable page 149. Session Two: fold six pieces of A4 card (so that each card can be placed over the back of a chair). Write a different village occupation on each card. Place six chairs around the edges of three sides of the room and space them out as evenly as possible. Session Three: organize the room so that groups of children can sit together, with the relevant history books and other resources.

Resources needed

Photocopiable page 149, information (books, CD-ROMs) about everyday occupations in a village or settlement of the chosen period, writing and drawing materials, six pieces of A4 card, six chairs, a whistle, a CD player or a cassette player, a recording of some music appropriate to the period, a scarf or a similar small item of clothing appropriate to the period.

What to do
Session One

Ask the children if, during the forthcoming drama lesson, they will take on the roles of adults who live and work in an imaginary village of the period. Organize the class into six groups and allocate each group a village occupation. Explain that the drama will begin on an ordinary working day in the village. Ask each group to find out what kind of work is involved in their occupation, using the information resources you have provided.

Give out copies of photocopiable page 149 and explain that the children should use the information they have found out to fill in their sheets. Make it clear that they must focus on the jobs they do, rather than trying to include everything that happens from the moment they wake up in the morning. Encourage group members to help each other with this task. When the sheets have been completed, ask the children to underline the task they intend to carry out first in the drama. Groups may wish to discuss this with each other first.

Session Two

Ask the children to sit on the floor in their groups, at the end of the room where there are no chairs. Place one occupation card on the back of each chair, round the edges of the room. Ask the class to imagine that the room represents the village in the drama. Explain that each chair

Now sit the children together in a large group in the centre of the village and restart the drama to hold a village meeting. Introduce an appropriate problem or event for the villagers to consider – for instance, a rumour might be going round a Victorian village that a railway is to be built in the village; a Tudor village might receive a message from a group of beggars, asking the village to act illegally by giving them food; a Celtic settlement might hear about the approaching Romans and must decide whether to run or stay and fight. Remain in the drama to discuss the problem. Try to open up possibilities and implications rather than seeking a definite decision in this session. Finally, ask the villagers to go away and think about the problem for a while, then stop the drama.

Session Three

Use history books and other resources to help the children to explore the nature and implications of the problem or event. Then ask the children to sit in their occupation groups. Ask the children to imagine that they are the villagers sitting together in their respective houses. On the word 'Action' they must come to life and talk about the problem.

Tell the children to start their improvisations by asking every member of the group to say what they think the village should do about the problem and why. Stop the improvisations when one or two groups appear to have finished.

Now ask groups to spend the next few minutes rehearsing a short version of their improvisations, so that they can perform them to the class. After the performances, ask the children to vote on which opinion they feel most sympathy with at the moment.

Finish the session by narrating what may have happened as a consequence of the different solutions and explore any other related issues. For example, if they were to vote

represents the back of a house and workplace. Define any areas or items in the room that are not to be used in the drama, for example wall bars or PE equipment.

Tell the children that they will need to mime everything they need for their occupations, and give a few examples by demonstrating. Make it clear that they will need to talk to each other as if they were the villagers. Remind the children that the drama will begin first thing in the morning, when everyone is ready to start work. Give the children a few minutes to discuss how they might mime their jobs and tell them to fold their arms when they are ready.

Tell the children that they may also visit other villagers in the drama to exchange things for goods, for example a carpenter might offer some firewood to a blacksmith in exchange for a tool.

Explain that whenever you wear the scarf you will be playing the role of one of the villagers, who makes a living by growing food or making things. Ask the children to imagine that they are actors in a video film about the period. Tell them that you will need them to start in a 'frozen position', as if the video was on a pause. Give the children a few minutes to decide on the positions they will take up, as they start their first job. Explain that when everyone is in position, you will say the word 'Action' and play some background music to bring the village to life. The drama should carry on until you blow the whistle and say 'Freeze', when they must stop.

Play the music and start the drama. Put on the scarf and visit each group, offering your produce in exchange for other goods. Let the drama run for as long as most children seem to be engaged. After stopping the drama, ask each group to sit in front of the chair that represents their house.

Ask three groups to show the other children some of the things they were doing in the village. Tell them to start with their original positions. Keep this short and then ask the other three groups to perform in the same way.

DRAMA

Opportunities for IT

Some children could use the computer to research information for Sessions One and Three. They could access either an encyclopaedia CD-ROM or specific CD-ROMs based on a particular period in history. Schools with access to the Internet or National Grid for Learning (NGFL) will be able to allow children to search for information online. You could also download information they have already found and save it on the hard drive of the computer or network so that children can access these materials without going online.

Children could also present their researched information using a word processor to form part of a class display about the period of history being studied.

Display ideas

The information on the photocopiable sheets can be displayed inside the outlines of six houses to represent the occupations. Some children can also draw a map of the village, as they imagine it to be, and this can be displayed alongside the sheets and their word-processed information on the period (see 'Opportunities for IT').

against building a railway that ran to their Victorian seaside village, then the village would not develop as a holiday resort.

Reference to photocopiable sheet

Photocopiable page 149 provides a framework for the research carried out during Session One. The sheet helps to focus the children's minds on the roles they will play, rather than just what their occupations are.

Suggestion(s) for extension

In Session One, encourage the children to carry out some or all of the research themselves and to make their roles as accurate as possible, based on the research. During Session Two, invite confident children to make constructive comments about the quality of the drama as performed by the other three groups. In Session Three challenge more confident children to make their improvised conversations more interesting, using pauses in the dialogue and incorporating changes in their physical positions.

Villager's role sheet

Name _____

Date _____

▲ Fill in the spaces.
In the drama I will play the part of someone called _____

Here are some details about my role:
I live in a village and my occupation is _____

My family consists of _____

For my main meal I eat _____

I sleep on _____

If I have any free time I like to _____

Here is a list of five jobs I do every day:

1 _____   4 _____

2 _____   5 _____

3 _____

The job I **enjoy** most is _____

The job I **dislike** most is _____

Here is a picture of me at work.

Here is a picture of where I live.

Suggestion(s) for support

The work in Session One can be simplified by asking children to choose one or two tasks from a list of possibilities for their occupation. Present the research material so that it is accessible for the less confident children and use plenty of visual images to support them in their understanding of their occupation. Make a simplified version of the photocopiable sheet, involving freehand drawings of the tasks or appropriate pictures that you have selected. Put less confident children in mixed-ability groups to support them during Sessions Two and Three.

Assessment opportunities

During Session One, assess children's study skills and their ability to write in role. During Sessions Two and Three, look for children who work collaboratively and speak with appropriate dialogue when in role.

TUTANKHAMUN

To re-enact aspects of a historical event from the perspective of participants.

†† *Whole class and groups.*

🕐 *45–60 minutes.*

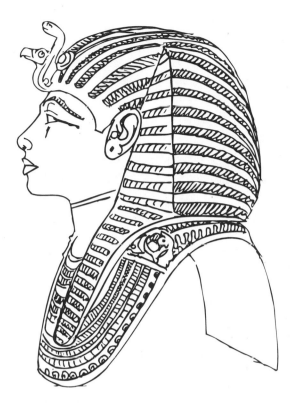

Previous skills/knowledge needed

Children should have some background knowledge about ancient Egypt and the tombs. They should know what an archaeologist is and how archaeologists excavated the tombs of ancient Egypt in the past. The drama works best if the children have not heard the story of Tutankhamun before.

Key background information

The drama seeks to give the children a sense of the excitement and anticipation felt by the people involved in the events of the discovery of the tomb of Tutankhamun in the 1920s. The re-enactment is designed to reveal the main events as they occur. Warn the children beforehand that some of them may have heard the story before. If you find that this is the case, ask them to keep it to themselves until the end of the drama, when they will be invited to compare their version of the story with the one in the drama. Use the words 'Action' and 'Freeze' to stop and start the drama each time.

Preparation

Make one copy per child of photocopiable page 150 (enlarged, if necessary). Place five chairs at one end of the room and arrange them as in the diagram below. Place the box of material and objects beside the chairs. Set up the CD/cassette player to play the music. Place the waistcoat or cravat at the opposite end of the room to the chairs.

Resources needed

A large space, a CD or cassette player, some slow, dreamy music (for example, *Glass Village* by Inner Sense Percussion), five chairs, a box containing two lengths of plain gold or shiny yellow material (each piece should measure about two metres in length), three or four plain golden items (such as gold chains, plain brass ornaments and containers), a man's waistcoat or cravat suited to the 1920s period, a whistle, pictures and other materials relating to the discovery of the tomb of Tutankhamun, photocopiable page 150, writing and drawing materials.

What to do

Organize the children so that they are sitting in small groups, as far away as possible from the arrangement of chairs. Ask them to take part in a re-enactment of a true story that happened in Egypt in the 1920s. Explain that they will play the parts of some archaeologists who arrived to help a man

called Howard Carter on a dig in the Valley of the Kings. Talk about the kind of environment in which they will be working. Ask them to imagine that the room represents a corner of the Valley of the Kings (tell them to keep away from the arrangement of chairs at the end of the room). Tell the children that when you are wearing the waistcoat or cravat, you will be playing the role of Howard Carter. Explain that you will not be attempting to speak in a different voice or look like Howard Carter and so you will use the clothing as a sign that you are in role.

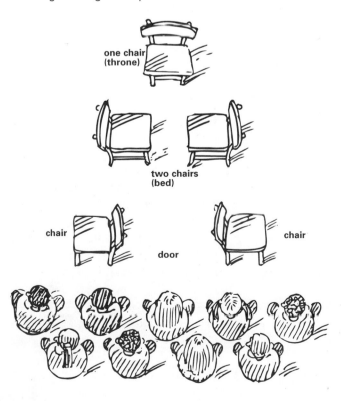

one chair
(throne)

two chairs
(bed)

chair   chair

door

Ask the class to imagine that they have just arrived at the base, with all their camping equipment and provisions. Make sure the children understand that the equipment would be the kind used in the 1920s. Explain that on the word 'Action', the drama will start at their first meeting with Howard Carter and it will finish when you say 'Freeze'.

Put on the clothing and greet the archaeologists as if you were Howard Carter. Tell them about the lost tomb of Tutankhamun and how you believe it to be in the last triangle of land as yet unexcavated in the Valley of the Kings. Tell them that Lord Carnarvon is financing the project and that this is your last chance to find the tomb. Describe what you think may be inside the tomb and then leave them with the words 'Tomorrow we start the dig'. Stop the drama and take off the clothing to come out of role.

Tell the children that the next time you say 'Action' they must play the parts of the archaeologists as they make camp. Define any areas of the room that are out of bounds for the drama and then explain that all their actions must be mimed. Give a few suggestions by demonstrating how

to mime putting in tent pegs and unpacking boxes. Make it clear that the children will work in their groups and will need to speak to each other as if they were really there. Tell the children that, after they have unpacked, they should find some firewood to make a fire and sit around their fires, warming their hands. Keep this section brief and do not go into role yourself unless you need to control the children or give them support. Stop the drama when you see a few groups sitting round their fires.

Explain that you will now move time on to the first day of the dig. When you restart the drama, the children should find their imaginary tools, stake out the land and carefully start the dig. Tell them that, because this is a true story, we

know that nothing was found on the first day and so they must not invent any interesting discoveries. Start the drama but keep this section brief. Again, do not go into role as Howard Carter unless you need to support less confident children.

Stop the drama and tell the children that by the end of the first day, nothing was found and the same thing happened on the second day. However, on the morning of the third day something happened. Tell the children that Howard Carter knew something had happened because when he came out of his tent that morning there was a strange silence, and when he looked for his workers they were standing round something in the ground.

To prepare for the next part of the drama, ask the children to stand in a large semicircle, as if they were looking at a point in the ground. Tell them that the archaeologists had found some steps, leading under the ground. Start the drama again at the point when Howard Carter talks to his archaeologists about the steps. In role as Carter, tell the archaeologists your excitement about the possibility that these steps might lead to a door to the tomb of Tutankhamun. Ask them to work slowly and carefully to uncover the rest of the steps, without damaging any door which may be at the bottom of the steps. Tell them to fetch their equipment and start work. Remain in role to supervise this activity and keep it short.

Stop the drama and tell the children to stand back in the semicircle and sit down. Explain that the archaeologists found sixteen steps and at the bottom of the sixteenth step they found a door. Howard Carter was reluctant to break through the door without Lord Carnarvon being there and so everyone had to wait for about three weeks for him to arrive. Tell the children that the door led to a passage under the ground which finally led to a second door.

Talk about what Howard Carter saw through the hole in the second door and describe what was in the chamber. Now ask the children to sit in front of the two chairs representing the entrance to the chamber. Ask them to imagine that the area behind the two chairs represents the inside of the chamber, and explain that you will use material and objects to indicate the gold colours there. Drape one length of material over the two chairs in the centre to make it look like the shape of an old-fashioned bed. Then drape the other piece of material over the chair at the back, to represent Tutankhamun's throne. Now place the objects on the bed and near the throne.

Explain that you would like the children to perform a reconstruction of what it might have been like when the archaeologists first broke into the chamber and took out the objects. Tell them that you will play some background music and then point to groups, one at a time, to go into the chamber area and pretend to bring out some objects. Ask each child to think of an object that they will bring out of the chamber. They should think about the size and weight of the object and then decide how they will mime picking it up and carrying it to their tent. Tell them to fold their arms when they have made these decisions.

Explain that each child should pick up their imaginary object and carefully take it back to their tent to brush off any dirt and examine it. They should then tell others in their tent what they have found and what else they saw in the chamber. Each group should then remain in their tent until you stop the drama. When everyone is ready, start the music and let groups take turns to move into the chamber to collect their imaginary objects and take them back to their tents. Stop the drama when the last group has completed the task.

Tell the children that because of the slow process of dealing with the objects and the sheer number of them, it took months before all the objects were removed. Ask them to imagine that it is now two weeks since they started to take objects out of the chamber, and explain that the drama will begin again with a meeting between Howard Carter and his team. Put on the clothing and take on the role of Howard Carter to address the meeting. Tell the archaeologists about the problems with the press and how they are getting in the way of the work by crowding round the entrance to the passage to take photographs. Suggest that they build a wall around the entrance to keep the press and the tourists back. Explain that hundreds of tourists are on their way to see the site and that you are concerned that they will be a nuisance. Tell the archaeologists to find some rocks and stones and build a wall around the entrance as soon as possible. Allow the children a few minutes to start to build the wall and then stop the drama.

Call the children back and tell them what happened when Howard Carter opened a third door at the back of the chamber. Tell them about the problems Howard Carter had with the Egyptian government and how he was ordered to leave just as he was about to discover the body of Tutankhamun. Explain that Howard Carter and his archaeologists were allowed back 18 months later. Ask those children who know the story if they can remember what was found.

Go back to the classroom and use the pictures and other information about the real discovery of the tomb of Tutankhamun to describe the details of what was subsequently found. Give each child a copy of photocopiable page 150, and explain each stage carefully. The first stage involves filling in the thought bubbles of the archaeologists, first as they look for the tomb and then as they wait for Lord Carnarvon; the second stage involves depicting the discovery of the objects (perhaps with the addition of thought bubbles); and the third stage involves writing appropriate thoughts for the press and tourists. Finally, ask some children to read out their thought bubbles to the class.

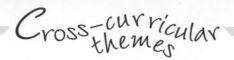

Suggestion(s) for extension

Most of this activity involves working as a whole group in short structured situations but during the section on reflection, more able children can work in small groups to produce a series of freeze-frames depicting the moments shown on the photocopiable sheet. They can then add their own spoken thoughts in the freeze-frames (see 'Significant moments' on page 18).

Alternatively, they can make up a short improvisation based on one of the moments on the sheet. Ask the children to look at evidence of the discovery to check for any inaccuracies in the drama.

Suggestion(s) for support

Put less confident children with those who are more confident when working in groups. Support children in the whole group mimes by directing them while in role as Howard Carter. For example, when the archaeologists are starting the dig, ask a less confident child or children to help you move some heavy rocks from one of the areas.

Assessment opportunities

Look for children who attempt to make their mime work convincing and those who use appropriate dialogue when in role.

Opportunities for IT

After the re-enactment, the children can use the computer to research information about Tutankhamun to extend their own knowledge and understanding. They could use an encyclopaedia CD-ROM or specific CD-ROMs based on the Ancient Egyptians. Some schools may even have access to newspaper CD-ROMs from that particular time. Schools with access to the Internet or National Grid for Learning (NGFL) will be able to allow children to search for information online. There are several excellent sites about ancient Egypt for children to explore.

If children are searching online they will need to be shown how to create a simple search using a search engine, how to narrow the search down using AND or + operators and how to quickly identify likely sites from the results of the search. They will also need to save the important pages to disk or print them out.

The children could present their findings using a word processor or desktop publishing program or even create their own Ancient Egyptian or Tutankhamun World Wide Web pages for other children to use in the future.

Some simulation software, such as Arc-Venture series by Sherston Software, encourages children to take on the roles of archaeologists in different periods of history. These simulations might be used alongside the drama activities to explore other aspects of archaeology and to enable children to discuss the benefits and limitations of this type of software.

Display ideas

Display the completed photocopiable sheets, or cut out some of the children's own pictures from the sheets and mount them on card, to display along with other information about the discovery of Tutankhamun.

Reference to photocopiable sheet

Photocopiable page 150 can be used to encourage the children to reflect on their thoughts and feelings when they were in role as archaeologists. It also reinforces knowledge of the main events in the story.

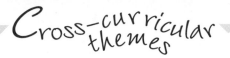

THESEUS AND THE MINOTAUR

To re-enact parts of a myth using whole-group drama, freeze-frames and spoken thoughts.

†† *Whole class, pairs and groups.*

🕐 *60 minutes.*

Previous skills/knowledge needed
Some previous experience in devising and performing freeze-frames in groups would be helpful. Children need to have some basic background knowledge about life in ancient Greece and should understand what a myth is. It is better if the children do not know the story of Theseus and the Minotaur prior to the drama.

Key background information
This activity helps to bring the myth of Theseus and the Minotaur to life by looking at parts of it from the perspective of some of the characters. It engages children with some of the events in an active way and tells the story through a combination of whole-group drama and narration. The lesson concludes with an exploration of the moral dimensions of the story, in terms of who is to blame for the death of King Aegeus. All these activities are designed to bring children into a personal relationship with the story to stimulate enjoyment, discussion and recall. It may also encourage children to read other versions of this particular myth and to read other Greek myths. Use the word 'Action' to start the drama and the word 'Freeze' to stop it each time.

Preparation
Select a space at the side of a large room, preferably near a wall bar if you are in the hall where PE is held, and big enough for all the children to sit together later on in the drama. Tie a piece of black material to the wall bar or stand a flip chart or an easel on the floor and drape the material over this instead. Place a chair near the black material. Fold up a white cotton sheet and place it under the chair. Make one copy per child of photocopiable page 151 . Collect as many versions of the myth of Theseus and the Minotaur as possible.

Resources needed
A large space, wall bar (or flip chart/easel), different versions of the story of Theseus and the Minotaur, photocopiable page 151, black cotton cloth (about two metres long), a white cotton sheet, a chair, a cloak or length of material to represent the role of Theseus, writing materials.

What to do
Put the children into mixed-ability groups, with about four in each group. Sit the groups together at the opposite side of the room but facing the black material. Tell them that the drama will be about a Greek myth that they may already know. If they know it, ask the children to keep it to themselves until after the first part of the drama. Explain that the story is about something that happened to a group of young adults who lived in Athens at the time of the ancient Greeks. Ask the children to play the parts of these young adults.

Ask them to imagine that they all received a message from King Aegeus, the king of Athens. The message was that they should go to the nearest harbour and look for a ship with a black sail. They were to wait by the ship for further instructions. Tell them that the black material represents the black sail and that the space near it represents the ship.

Explain that at the start of the drama, they will be asked to load the ship with boxes of provisions and barrels of water that are stored near the ship. Tell the children that they will need to mime this, and talk about how to mime carrying things of different weights and sizes. Suggest that they mime rolling the barrels onto the ship because of the weight.

Tell the children that as the young adults sat by the ship, a young man came over to talk to them. The man was Prince Theseus, son of King Aegeus of Athens. Explain that when you put on the cloak, you will play the part of Theseus, but you will not be attempting to look like Theseus or talk in a different voice. (Alternatively, you could narrate what Theseus told the young Greeks, instead of speaking in role.)

Put on the cloak and play the role of Theseus. Ask the children if they are the young people sent by your father to meet by the ship with the black sail. Tell them that you cannot reveal why they have been called here until you are all on the ship. Then add that they are about to go on a long journey and should load the ship with as many boxes of provisions and barrels of water as it will take. Promise to tell them what this is all about after the ship has set sail. Tell them to load the ship immediately and then move on to the ship to direct the proceedings. After a short while, sit on the chair and call the young people to sit with you. Explain that as the ship has now set sail, you will tell them why they are here.

Tell the story in your own words, as if you were Theseus, as in the following example.

I shall now tell you why you are here. When I tell you this, please do not be frightened, because I have a plan that will save us.

I shall begin at the beginning. It all started a long time ago, when you and I were children. My father held some games here in Athens and people came from other areas to take part. Across the sea there is an island called Crete. The King of Crete is called King Minos and he sent his only son to take part in the games. This young man was so good that he won nearly every event. Then something terrible happened. Someone from this city of Athens was so jealous of this young man that they murdered him. King Minos was so angry that he threatened to wage war on Athens and kill us all. King Minos was very powerful and my father knew that if he carried out his threat, we would all die. My father asked King Minos if there was anything he could do to prevent him from attacking Athens.

It was then that King Minos and my father made the deal. Apparently, in Crete there is a creature known as the Minotaur. It has the head and body of a huge bull and the legs of a man and it lives underground in a labyrinth of tunnels. Every nine years the Minotaur comes out of the labyrinth looking for food. The Minotaur likes to eat young humans and every nine years it kills large numbers of young people from Crete. King Minos said that if my father sent a boatload of our young people to Crete every nine years, to be fed to the Minotaur instead of the people of Crete, he would not attack Athens. My father had to agree. King Minos wanted to know how he would know which boat from Athens would be the one containing the young people to be sacrificed to the Minotaur and my father said: 'You will know the ship… it will be the ship of death… and it will be flying a black sail…'

I am sorry, but this is the ship and you are the young people to be sent into the labyrinth to meet the Minotaur, but do not worry for I have a plan and I will kill the Minotaur, before it kills us. I have made my father a promise that if I kill the Minotaur, he will know as soon as he sees our ship approaching because I will take down the black sail of death and replace it with this white sail (bring out the white sheet from under the chair).

After telling the story, stop the drama, take off the cloak and ask the children how they felt as the young Greeks when they heard what Theseus had to say. Talk about whether anyone felt angry or betrayed and whether they felt that Theseus would succeed in killing the Minotaur.

Now tell the children how Ariadne gave Theseus some magic thread and a sword to kill the Minotaur. Ask two members of the class to represent this moment in a freeze-frame, using suggestions made by the class on where and how they would be positioned and how they would look. Then ask the class to suggest what each character might be thinking at this moment. Ask the characters to make

Suggestion(s) for extension
When making the freeze-frame about leaving Ariadne, ask more able groups to bring their freeze-frame to life and to include a conversation between the young people about the situation.

Suggestion(s) for support
Work with less confident groups to help them produce the freeze-frame about leaving Ariadne. Encourage the children to keep their spoken thoughts simple or omit the thoughts altogether. Let children work with a more able partner to fill in their sheets, or make a simplified version by reducing the number of sentences and simplifying the vocabulary. When discussing the issue of blame, differentiate through questioning to support those who need it.

Assessment opportunities
Look for children who listen carefully to the storytelling and note those who invent appropriate thoughts for the freeze-frames. Look for children who show an awareness of the moral issues of the story through their contributions to the final discussion.

Performance ideas
Use the sentences on photocopiable page 151 as a basis for performing the story through a series of freeze-frames, linked together by a narrator.

Reference to photocopiable sheet
Photocopiable page 151 provides a focus for reflection on the events and moral implications in the story. It gives the children time to consider the issues, before being asked to discuss them, and gives them an opportunity to recall the main events of the story before being asked to make comparisons with other versions.

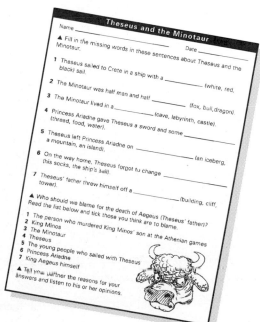

the freeze-frame again, but this time speaking their thoughts out loud.

Next, tell the children about how Theseus killed the Minotaur. Ask two children to represent the Minotaur on the ground and another to represent Theseus, about to cut off its head. Make this into a freeze-frame without the spoken thoughts.

Tell the children about how Ariadne stowed away on the returning ship and was discovered when the ship sheltered on an island during a storm. Explain how Theseus and the young Athenians left Ariadne asleep on the island because she wanted to marry Theseus and be queen of Athens. Put the children into their groups and tell each group to prepare a freeze-frame of the moment when Theseus and the young people left Ariadne asleep on the island. Tell them to include their thoughts at this time. When the freeze-frames have been completed, let the children perform them to the rest of the class.

Now tell the children about how Theseus forgot to change the sail and how Aegeus thought that his son was dead and threw himself off the cliff. Ask two children to make a freeze-frame with spoken thoughts, to depict the moment when Theseus found his father's body on the shore and realized that he had not changed the sail.

Give out copies of photocopiable page 151. Ask the class to fill in the sheets to remind them of the story and think about who was responsible for the king's death. Put the children into pairs to discuss their answers. Then come together as a class and share ideas about the death of the king and who should take the blame. Finally, look at other versions of the myth and make comparisons.

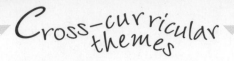

THE ROMAN ROAD

To increase an understanding of historical events through role-play and teacher-in-role.

†† *Groups and pairs.*

🕐 *30 minutes.*

Previous skills/knowledge needed

The children should have some background knowledge about Roman Britain and how the Romans built their roads.

Key background information

This activity uses drama to inform children about different Celtic responses to the coming of the Romans. It requires the children to impart this information to a Roman soldier who is unaware of the situation, thus creating the opportunity for recall and reinforcement. It makes use of teacher-in-role as the central teaching strategy. Use the words 'Action' and 'Freeze' to start and stop the drama each time.

Resources needed

A large space, a whistle, a PE band to wear across the chest to represent the role of a soldier, a woollen cloak or small blanket in a dark colour to represent the role of a Celt.

What to do

Put the children into pairs, within four mixed-ability groups. Number the groups one to four. Ask the children if they will play the parts of Roman soldiers building a road to the North of England. Explain that each group will be responsible for a particular part of the road-building process. The soldiers will work in pairs on their jobs. Talk about what tasks would be involved and share these out among the four groups. Tell the children that they will need to mime the tasks but they will be expected to talk to each other as if they were soldiers building the road.

Ask the class to imagine that the centre of the room is a piece of land. Explain that this is where they will be building the road. Give pairs a few minutes to decide which job they will start with and tell them to fold their arms when they have decided. Allocate one part of the room as the base for each group and ask them to stand in their areas, ready to start. Explain that you will start the drama with the word 'Action' and stop the drama by blowing the whistle and saying 'Freeze'.

Start the drama and let it run for a few minutes. Then tell the children to sit in their group areas in the room. Ask them to imagine that they are to receive a visit from a Roman officer, who is to inspect the road building. Explain that when you put on the band, you will play the part of this officer. Set the children to work as the soldiers once more and then put on the band to play the part of the officer. Walk around asking the soldiers questions about their work and then call them to stand in a line at one side of the room.

Tell them that they are doing a good job on the road, but there is trouble with the Picts and Scots in the north. Explain that the road must be built quickly so that more soldiers can go north to fight. Tell the soldiers that they should ask some of the local Celts to help them build the road. Explain how some of the Celts are keen to have the roads built so that they can use them for trade. Talk about how most of the Celts are grateful for all the Romans have done. Tell the soldiers that many Celts have jobs in the new Roman towns and many are grateful for peace in the land since the Romans came. Tell the soldiers to find some Celts to work with them as soon as possible, and then stop the drama.

Tell the children that when you put on the cloak, you will play the part of a Celt who has come to look at the road

building. Explain that when the drama starts, the soldiers should resume their work and when the Celt arrives, they should stop work and ask to speak to him. Choose one child to be the soldier who will ask the Celt if everyone can speak to him. Then decide on where you will all sit to talk. Remind them that they must ask the Celts for help with the road.

Start the drama and after a short while, enter as the Celt and wait for the soldier to approach you, as arranged. Sit with the soldiers and ask them why the road needs to be built so quickly. Tell them that some Celts might help them, including yourself, but warn them that there are other Celts who are angry that the Romans have taken over Britain. Tell them about the stories you have heard about Boudicca and the fighting in London, Colchester and St Albans and warn them to be on their guard. Offer to go back to your village and ask the Celts if any of them will work on the roads. Then stop the drama.

Talk about the situation out of role. Discuss whether the soldiers would trust the Celts and how the soldiers could best prevent being attacked as they build the road. Start the drama again as the soldiers sit in groups of four or five and share ideas on how to protect themselves.

After a while, put on the band and come into the drama as the officer. Ask the soldiers why they are not working and ask them if they have contacted the Celts. Encourage the soldiers to tell you about the threats and then tell them that those Celts who will not help with the road will be forced to do so and treated as slaves. Explain that Romans must be strong or they will lose power. Reassure the soldiers that there are only a few Celts who are against them and they just need to keep their eyes open for trouble as they work. Instruct the soldiers to go back to work and stop the drama after a short period.

Talk about how the events in the drama relate to what we know about the response of the Celts to the Romans.

Finally, ask the children if they would help the Romans build the roads if they were a Celt.

Suggestion(s) for extension
Listen in to the soldiers' conversations as they sit around talking about how to protect themselves from the Celts and identify the more confident groups. Ask these groups to hold a version of their conversation again, so that the class can listen in.

Suggestion(s) for support
Put less confident children in pairs with those who are more confident and will support them. Differentiate through questioning during the class discussions.

Assessment opportunities
Look for children who attempt to make their mimes accurate and respond appropriately in role. Note those who are able to discuss the issues confidently, both in and out of role.

Opportunities for IT
Children could use the computer to research information about Roman roads. They could use either an encyclopaedia CD-ROM or specific CD-ROMs based on the Romans. Schools with access to the Internet or National Grid for Learning (NGFL) will be able to allow children to search for information online. You could also download information they have already found and save it on the hard drive of the computer or on the network so that children can access these materials without going online.

Performance ideas
Organize the road-building mimes into a sequence of movements and develop them into a dance drama for a short performance.

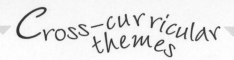

PRIDE OF PLACE

To build confidence in using persuasive vocabulary and images within a dramatic context.

✠ *Whole class and groups.*

🕐 *45–60 minutes.*

Previous skills/knowledge needed

The children need to have some knowledge of their locality in terms of facilities and areas of interest. Some previous experience in working out short improvisations and freeze-frames in small groups would be helpful (see 'Significant moments' on page 18).

Key background information

This activity offers children the opportunity to work in ability groups to produce a piece of drama suited to their levels of confidence in performance. The groups are asked to be selective and present a biased view in favour of their local area for an imaginary television show. This can help children to identify biased reports in the media in general.

Preparation

Make one copy per child of photocopiable page 152. If you are using a video camera, set this up to be ready for the last 15 minutes of the lesson.

Resources needed

A small space for each group to practise a scene, photocopiable page 152, writing materials, flip chart or board, a video camera (optional).

What to do

Put the children into ability groups according to their confidence in performance, with about four in each group. Ask them to pretend that they are making a video for an imaginary television programme called 'Pride of Place'. Viewers are asked to send in videos to convince a panel of judges that their local area is a place of which they can be proud. The best place, in the opinion of the judges, will win some money to spend on the children of the area.

Explain that in order to identify the best aspects of where they live and to make sure that they avoid the worst things, they should fill in a confidential form which will give the true picture of their area. The children must then select the best things about their area for the video and ignore the bad things. Give out copies of photocopiable page 152 and ask the children to complete it. When a few children have finished, stop the activity and write a list on the board of all the positive things that the children have identified about their area.

Tell the children that they must now bring these positive things about the area to life for the imaginary video. This will be achieved by pretending to record conversations and interviews and taking still pictures and films of events. Explain that the video must present a wonderful picture of the area, which may mean that they need to exaggerate the good things and avoid the bad. Discuss a few possibilities, such as interviewing someone who has lived in the area for years and loves it, or acting out a conversation between parents at the park talking about how their children love the swings. Other ideas could include an imaginary film showing people tending their gardens and a picture freeze-frame of a local sporting event. List some possibilities in note form on the board and explain that each group will present a different item from the list. Allocate these according to the children's abilities, keeping the freeze-frames and mimes for the less confident children.

Give the children a time-limit of about ten to fifteen minutes to produce their dramas in rough outline. If one or two groups finish well before the others ask them to prepare a second similar item for the video. Gather the class together and ask them to show the others either the finished drama or work in progress.

Explain that you will be providing the voice-over to link all the items together. Discuss the best order of presentation for the items and then ask the children for advice on the first and last thing that should be said on the video – the words must be chosen carefully to create a good impression. Write these down on the board.

Give groups a few minutes to polish up or complete their item and then organize an imaginary video shoot. If you are using a real video camera, use it at this point. Perform the items in the agreed order and link them with narration, using the children's suggestions for the first and last lines. Then give each group a few minutes to identify the aspect of their performance they would most like to improve and ask them to share their thoughts with the class.

Conclude by asking the children to imagine that they won the competition and had to decide how best to spend the prize money on the children of the area. Ask the children for some suggestions. Talk about whether the video would present a true picture of the area and ask them what key information was missing from the video, if any. Relate this to how tourist brochures try to attract visitors.

Suggestion(s) for extension
Ask the more able groups to work on the improvised conversations and the interviews and encourage them to invent interesting characters and situations.

Suggestion(s) for support
Pair up less confident children with those who are more confident when completing the photocopiable sheets. Ask less confident groups to make up freeze-frames or mimes and give them particular support at the preparation session, so that they are clear what the end-product will look like.

Assessment opportunities
Look for children who appreciate the need for bias when preparing their items for the video. Note those children who reveal a sense of audience by trying to make their video contribution suitable for the purpose.

Opportunities for IT
If a real video camera is available, children can take it in turns to use the camera to record the different items. The children could also record the interviews using a cassette player. The work could be presented using a multimedia authoring package in which children can display their freeze-frames and add sounds recorded with a microphone connected to the computer as well as additional text or pictures to explain their work.

This project could be linked to other work on the locality and include photographs of places in the locality taken with a digital camera, or scanned from photographs. A title page could list each of the different places so that when children select a particular place they see a freeze-frame or video film, with narration heard in the background. Other choices on the page might take children to other pictures of the locality and give relevant information about each place.

Children could also use a word processor or desktop publishing package to create a holiday-style brochure about the locality, highlighting the good features. An appropriate layout for this work would be an A4 sheet folded into three sections vertically, each section containing a mixture of text and pictures and the first section incorporating the title. Children could also add text from parts of their recorded interviews, perhaps using speech bubbles to highlight people's views of the locality. Pictures could be taken using a digital camera or they could be scanned from photographs.

Performance ideas
The end-product of this lesson involving the voice-over and the video extracts can be polished up and rehearsed to make a live performance. Children can be encouraged to edit parts of their work and practise lines to ensure a smooth running order and good voice projection.

DRAMA

Pride of place

Name _____

Date _____

▲ Circle the facilities that are available in your local area.

health centre
supermarket   dentist   hairdresser
sports centre   lake or river   seashore
post office   swimming pool   small shops
telephone box   library   school
railway station   bus stop   children's park
                   café   restaurant

▲ Tick the statements that apply to your area.
1 Most people are friendly.
2 The countryside around here is beautiful.
3 Most people keep themselves to themselves.
4 Children have nowhere to play.
5 The area is usually clean and free of litter.
6 Some parts of the area are full of litter.
7 There is very little vandalism here.
8 The streets are quiet and peaceful in the evenings.
9 Children here are mostly well-behaved when they are out.
10 This is a busy area and young people have lots to do.
11 You can always find a shop open somewhere in the area.
12 You can get a bus or a train easily.

▲ What are the **two** best things about your area? Say why you have chosen these things.

Reference to photocopiable sheet

Photocopiable page 152 is used to help the children assess existing features of their local area and seeks to suggest a number of different opinions. It requires the children to answer the questions truthfully, so that they can make their biased version substantially different for the video task.

 ## OAKTON THEME PARK

To build confidence in playing two opposing roles within the same dramatic context.

†† *Whole class and groups.*

🕐 *60 minutes for each session.*

Previous skills/knowledge needed

The children should know what a theme park is.

Key background information

This activity involves three sessions; the time between each session should ideally be no longer than a week. The first session helps the children establish their roles as members of an imaginary community, while Session Two allows them to take on very different roles within the same drama. The third session divides the children into two groups, as the two roles come face to face in a situation of conflict.

The three sessions take the children through a number of different drama strategies, ranging from whole-group meetings in role, interviewing a teacher-in-role and freeze-frames to small group improvisations. Use the words 'Action' and 'Freeze' to start and stop the drama each time.

Preparation

Session One: make one copy per child of photocopiable page 153. Ensure that there is enough space for each group of three to practise a freeze-frame (see 'Significant moments' on page 18). Session Two: make one copy per child of photocopiable page 154. Sessions Two and Three: arrange the chairs in a semicircle.

Resources needed

A large space for Session Two, photocopiable pages 153 and 154, writing materials, flip chart or board, one chair per child plus one spare chair.

What to do
Session One

Put the children into threes. Ask the children if they will play the parts of some adults who live in an imaginary village called Oakton. Give out one copy per child of photocopiable page 153 and ask the children to look at the first section showing the map. Explain that they will live in one of three places: the new housing estate, the old housing estate or the cottages. Tell the children that they will be allowed to choose one of these three places after you have given them some information about the village, as written in the Newbry and District Visitors' Guide. Read out the extract as follows:

Oakton is a small but attractive village, about 15 miles from the town of Newbry. It gained its name from the old oak tree near the pond on the village green. The village is surrounded by farmland and is a quiet, peaceful place. Apart from a few shops, there is little work for the residents of Oakton and those who do work tend to work in Newbry. Although the motorway lies only five miles from Oakton via Oakton Road, driving along this road is not recommended. Oakton Road has several sharp bends and is very narrow – also, the surface of the road is very bumpy in places.

The village is dominated by the privately owned Oakton Hall, which has belonged to the Jackman family for generations. Once a year, the Hall grounds are opened to the public, revealing some attractive old woods and a beautiful lake. Lord Ronald Jackman and his wife Lady Susan still live in part of the Hall.

There are three main residential areas in Oakton. The terraced cottages are listed buildings and have been renovated to provide cosy accommodation with beautiful views over the green. The old housing estate consists of a range of detached and semi-detached houses with large well-established gardens. The new housing estate consists of a number of recently built houses and bungalows with ample car-parking space but small gardens.

Oakton has its own small primary school and a small church. There is a daily bus service to Newbry which runs every hour from 7am to 9pm.

Now ask the class to imagine they are the villagers and to think about what they value most about living in Oakton. Ask for suggestions and write these on the board. Expect things relating to the facilities such as the shops and school but try to encourage the children to consider things such as the peace and the beauty of the village.

Explain to the children that there is a plaque in the church which lists the most important events in the history of Oakton from 1700 to last year. The list includes both good and bad events, such as success in sporting events, disasters, crimes, visits to Oakton by famous people, competition winners and new projects in the village. Ask the children to work in their groups to make up two or three items that could be written on the plaque. They can make up anything they like as long as it is feasible. They should start with the date and then add a short sentence, choosing words that would be used on the plaque. Give the children a few examples, such as:

1922 Lord Ronald Jackman born at Oakton Hall
1974 Severe storm damaged Oakton church spire
1977 Oakton won the 'Best kept village competition'

When every group has thought of at least one idea, stop the activity and tell each group to pick out one of their ideas for the plaque. Then write the children's ideas in sentences on the board, in date order if possible.

Tell the class that the villagers of Oakton decided to make a tourist brochure of their own instead of relying on the Newbry and District Guide. They decided that the picture on the front cover should show people on the village green. Ask the children to suggest what the people in the picture could be doing. Use some or all of the class to make up a freeze-frame to depict this picture on the green.

Now ask the children to work in groups to prepare more freeze-frames to represent the photographs or pictures inside the brochure. The pictures could be real photographs or artists impressions. Explain that if children want to depict events from the plaque in the church, then they will need to represent artists impressions because they happened a long time ago. Explain that the pictures should indicate something of interest about Oakton, which will attract the visitors. Encourage groups to make just one or two good freeze-frames and tell them to invent a suitable caption to

DRAMA

go with each picture. When groups have prepared at least one freeze-frame, let them perform these to each other.

Go back to the copies of photocopiable page 153 and ask each child to fill in the section about their role as a villager. When most children have completed the sheets, ask each child to read out their new name, where they live in Oakton and what they like best and least about living in Oakton. Remind the children to write their real names on the sheets, before handing them in.

Session Two

Put the children into small groups with a maximum of five in each group. Ask everyone to take on their roles as Oakton villagers. Explain that they are at a meeting to discuss the village fête, which is usually held on the village green. Tell the children that for this part of the drama you will play the role of a villager who has been given the job of organizing the fête. Ask them to imagine that they have all volunteered to help at the fête, which is in three months' time.

Welcome the villagers to the meeting and explain that you have received an offer from Lord and Lady Jackman to hold this year's village fête in the grounds of Oakton Hall. Ask the villagers what they feel about this and either make a decision or ask them to think about it for the next meeting. Ask the villagers what attractions they would like to see at the fête and then decide who will be responsible for each activity on the day.

Stop the drama and explain that you will now take the drama forward to the day of the fête. The drama will begin an hour before the fête opens, as the villagers prepare their stalls and attractions. Allocate an area of the room for each attraction and ask the children to stand in the area in which they will work. Move the chairs to the sides of the room if

necessary. Emphasize that the children will be preparing for the visitors and not acting out the fête. Start the drama as the children mime making their preparations and talk to each other about the day. Let this run for a few minutes and then ask the children to sit back in the semicircle of chairs.

Ask the children to take on a different role for the next part of the drama. (Explain that they will be going back to their roles as villagers after this section.) Ask them to take on the roles of directors and managers of a construction company that builds leisure centres and theme parks. Explain that the company is called RC Construction and they have recently been in the papers because they are heavily in debt. They are looking for a site to build a new theme park to save the company from ruin. Ask the children to imagine that they are in a meeting to discuss the future of the company and stress that they should imagine that they know nothing about Oakton, which is about 50 miles away from the company headquarters. Tell the children that you will play the part of the Managing Director who will lead the meeting.

Welcome the directors to the meeting and tell them that you have some good news. You have found a site for the new theme park, but the owner of the land has not yet accepted your offer and so details should be kept secret for now. Explain that you are sure that the owner will sell because you have offered a large sum of money, which you are not allowed to disclose until the accountants confirm the exact figure.

Give out copies of photocopiable page 154 and explain that Oakton is a tiny village with no other theme park nearby and it is only five miles from a motorway. Tell them that the land for sale is owned by Lord and Lady Jackman. Refer to the sheet and talk about the proposed alterations to the site as shown in the striped area. The road will be widened all the way to the motorway to carry the coaches of visitors. The rear of the land will be developed into a car park and picnic area. Talk about benefits of the theme park to the village, such as more tourists in their shops and jobs for the villagers. Ask the directors to predict what objections the villagers might have to their plans. Explain that the company will be offering the farmers a good price for their land so that the alterations can be made. Offer to pass any financial questions they might have on to the company accountant.

Consider each objection and then ask the directors if they can think of anything the company can do or offer to defuse the objection. If the children find this difficult, then make suggestions yourself and invite their comments. For example, if the children pick out the fact that the tree will be under the new road and will die, suggest replanting it elsewhere or planting a new one. After some discussion, tell the directors that if this goes ahead, you plan to arrange a meeting with the villagers to persuade them not to object to the plans. Stop the drama and collect in the sheets.

Ask the children to sit in their small groups and to resume their roles as villagers. Tell them to imagine that they were invited to a meeting at the village hall to find out how much money was made for charity at the fête. On that same day, an advert had appeared in a national paper, advertising Oakton Hall for sale to the highest offer. A rumour was also going round that Oakton Hall might be bought by a company building a theme park. Give the children a minute to think in silence about how their role would feel about the prospect of a theme park. Then tell them to talk about the theme park with their group, as if they were the villagers at the village hall. They should make sure that they ask everyone in their group for their opinion. Warn them that they should stop talking when you arrive in role as the villager who organized the fête. Arrange to say a key phrase so that the children know when to stop talking in their groups, for example: 'Sorry I'm late… can we gather round to start the meeting please…'

In role as the fête organizer, announce that the fête made £150 for charity and then ask them what they were so busy talking about when you came in. Explain that you have not heard the rumours and use this to open up a general discussion about the matter. Suggest that they should arrange to see Lord or Lady Jackman to see if the rumours are true. Stop the drama.

Session Three

Place an empty chair in front of the class. Ask the children to imagine that a meeting was arranged with either Lord or Lady Jackman and tell the children that you will play this role when you sit on the empty chair. Ask them to consider the best way of starting the conversation with Lord or Lady Jackman and choose one child to make the first approach. Make it clear that after this child has spoken any child can speak. Ask them to put their hands up to ask questions if you have a large class.

Sit on the chair and conduct the interview. Take a civil but aloof attitude in this role. Reveal that costs of running Oakton Hall are too high and you need the money from the sale of Oakton Hall to start a new business elsewhere.

Make it clear that you are open to offers for another two weeks. Keep the interview short and then close the proceedings by telling the villagers that you have to leave for an important appointment elsewhere.

Tell the children that you want them to improvise the meeting between the villagers and RC Construction about the proposed theme park. Explain that the deal has still not been signed but the company wants to stop any bad publicity caused by the rumours. Ask up to six children to play the parts of representatives of RC Construction at the meeting. The rest of the class will play the villagers or the press.

Give everyone a few minutes to talk in pairs or groups to prepare what they will say at the meeting. Ask the children who will play the company representatives to predict what they will be asked and then prepare some suitable replies. Members of the press should be asked to prepare leading questions.

After the preparations, chair the meeting in role as the villager who organized the fête. Insist on a hands-up procedure to defuse any emotion and keep control. Stop the drama when most of the main points have been discussed. Summarize points throughout the meeting and ask questions yourself if necessary.

Tell the children that after the meeting, Lord and Lady Jackman sold their land to an organization called the National Properties Charity. This organization aims to preserve interesting properties for the public to enjoy. Explain that after the sale, the NPC wrote a letter to the villagers asking them what they would like to see happen to Oakton Hall and grounds. Conclude the activity by asking the children to discuss how they would reply to this letter.

Suggestion(s) for extension

Session One: ask the children to make an estate agent's leaflet about their house, after completing a copy of photocopiable page 153. Encourage them to include the peace and quiet of the village as a selling point. Session Two: direct probing questions at more confident children during the RC Construction meeting, to encourage them to explain and justify their responses to the new proposals. Session Three: choose the more confident children to play the roles of company representatives or members of the press at the meeting. The representatives should be encouraged to predict the questions they will be asked and to think of appropriate responses. The press should be encouraged to think of leading questions that will help them to sensationalize the story.

Suggestion(s) for support

Session One: put less confident children into mixed-ability groups to complete the tasks. Children who are unable to complete the written part of photocopiable page 153 can be asked to draw a picture of their character with a smile or a frown on the character's face to indicate how the person feels about living in Oakton. Session Two: put less confident children in pairs with those who will support them when working at the fête. Differentiate through questioning at the company meeting. Session Three: put less confident children with one or two others when preparing the questions for the meeting and allow them to stay in their original roles as the villagers.

Children could also use an art or drawing package to create posters advertising the fête or the other village activities. Some children might like to use a drawing or mapping package to make up a plan of the village showing the important features and where the proposed theme park will be.

Performance ideas

The improvisation of the meeting in Session Three that involved the discussion of the rumours that the villagers had heard can be refined and rehearsed for a performance to the class.

Display ideas

Some children may like to paint or draw suggestions for the front cover of the Oakton tourist brochure to put on display with a copy of the map.

Reference to photocopiable sheets

Photocopiable page 153 provides a map of the village and a framework to enable children to invent the key details about their roles as villagers and their likes and dislikes concerning the village. Photocopiable page 154 is used as a document in the company meeting. The document provides a visual focus to stimulate the discussion.

Assessment opportunities

Look for children who are able to change roles convincingly and with ease – those who are able to express views about the situation from the perspective of a company director as well as from the perspective of their village character. Note those children who are able to ask appropriate questions within a number of dramatic frameworks.

Opportunities for IT

This activity contains several opportunities for using a word processor. Children could:

▲ write and format the list of items on the memorial plaque, experimenting with different font styles to make the plaque look authentic; if there are lots of entries, a book could be produced which logs the village's history over a given period of time.

▲ create an advertising poster for the village meeting with the construction company

▲ write a letter to the National Properties Charity, explaining how the villagers would like the land to be used

▲ write an estate agent's account of Oakton Hall, or any of the other village properties

▲ design posters showing the villagers' feelings about the proposed theme park

▲ write letters about the proposed theme park to the local Newbry paper's letters column.

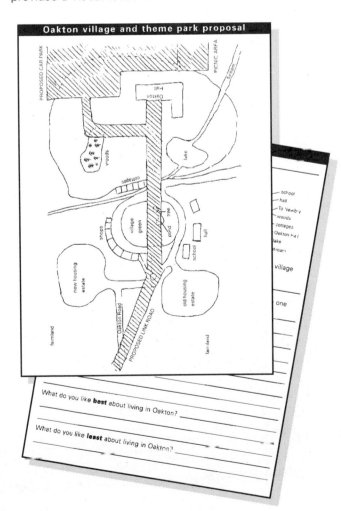

Oakton village and theme park proposal

LAKESIDE CAMP

To encourage roles of responsibility and problem-solving within a whole-group drama.

†† *Whole class and small groups.*

🕐 *Session One: 45 minutes. Session Two: 45 minutes.*

Previous skills/knowledge needed

The children should be familiar with the facilities on offer on a large family campsite. Familiarity with making freeze-frames (see 'Significant moments' on page 18) would be helpful.

Key background information

This activity gives children roles of responsibility as workers on a campsite. The problems require children to hold discussions in role and use mime to carry out any practical solutions to these problems. The activity has the potential for artwork as well as written work between the two sessions when children make an information centre for the campsite. The information centre could contain details of the facilities, along with grid-referenced routes on how to locate them, rules of the site and souvenir postcards of the lake. Use the words 'Action' and 'Freeze' to start and stop the drama each time.

Preparation

Session One: make one copy of photocopiable page 155 for each group. Draw a large copy of the campsite map as in the diagram below. Clip the map to a flip chart or an easel. Session Two: fix the map to the flip chart at one end of the room and place one small, blue, non-slip PE mat in the centre of the room.

Resources needed

Photocopiable page 155, writing materials, a large sheet of white paper, flip chart or easel, two bulldog clips, a small, blue, non-slip PE mat, a sheet of writing paper, a large space and a whistle for Session Two.

What to do
Session One

Organize the children into mixed-ability groups, with three in each group. Ask the children if, during the forthcoming drama lesson, they will play the roles of people who have just bought a large campsite as a business. Put the large map where everyone can see it. Explain that this is a sketch map of the site, as it is now, with very few facilities. Tell the children that the previous owners had not made a success of the business, due to the lack of facilities for campers. Invite the children to add some more facilities to the site, before the drama lesson. Discuss some possibilities and list them at the side of the map.

Then share out the facilities so that every group is made responsible for at least one facility. Now ask each group to decide where they would like to site their facility on the map. Ask one person from each group to write the name of their facility in the appropriate place on the map.

Give out one copy of photocopiable page 155 per group and ask the children to complete the sheet together. When most groups have finished the third section, stop the class

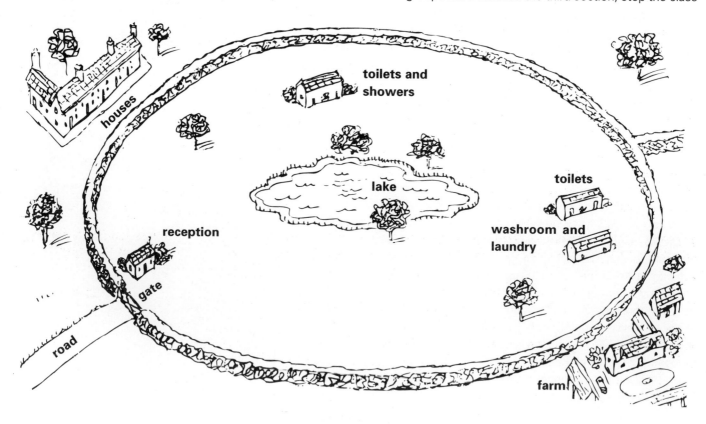

and let the groups show their freeze-frames and read out their captions to each other. Then let them resume work to complete their sheets.

Session Two

Place the blue mat in the centre of the room to represent the lake. Ask the children to sit at one end of the room, and fix the large map to the flip chart, to the side of the group. Ask the children to imagine that the mat represents the lake and the room represents the rest of Lakeside Camp. Define the areas of the room that are to be used in the drama. Ask groups to look at the map and then to sit in the place where their facility would be positioned in the room.

Explain that the drama will start early in the morning, before most campers are up. This is the time when the workers need to carry out some of their jobs. Give the groups a few minutes to decide what jobs they will do at this time of the day and tell them to fold their arms when they have decided.

Tell the children that when the drama begins, they should stand up and start to mime their jobs. Make it clear that they will be expected to talk to each other as if they really were the workers carrying out the jobs. Discuss some ways of miming a few jobs and then start the drama. Let this run for a few minutes or until some children begin to lose concentration.

Call the children together and ask them to imagine that they are at an owner's meeting on the site. Tell them that you will play the part of the owner who chairs the meetings and acts as the publicity agent. Start the drama by telling the other owners that you have some bad news. The police

have been to see you because several campers have had things stolen from their tents and caravans. The police think that the thieves are from the nearby village and they suggested that the owners make the campsite more secure. Ask for suggestions and discuss each suggestion in terms of it being legal, achievable and suited to the camp environment. For example, building a camp jail for suspected thieves would not be legal or achievable and would not look good in the brochure! Decide on some practical measures, such as putting up a fence or lighting the area at night, and then stop the drama.

Now ask the children to imagine that they have all the equipment they need to set up or make these changes and ask them to work on them on the site, using mime as before. Restart the drama and let it run for a few minutes before stopping and calling the children back to the meeting place.

Use the same format as the first meeting and present the children with some more problems. These can be reported by yourself or written in the form of an imaginary letter of complaint. Problems could include the following:
▲ A family complain that the open lake is dangerous for young children and demand that the owners find a way to make it safe.

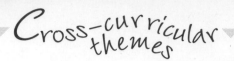
▲ Neighbouring farmers complain that some campers are damaging crops and leaving gates open, letting animals onto the road.

▲ Some campers are annoying people in nearby houses by making too much noise at night.

Look for practical solutions that can be carried out in mime or composed in writing as a group, but encourage the children to think through their ideas to ensure that they are feasible. For example, changes to campsite rules might be necessary to curb boisterous or inconsiderate campers. The children then need to consider how they can enforce these rules realistically, without breaking the law. Rules can be agreed and then put up in strategic places throughout the camp, using mime.

Conclude the drama by discussing how far the problems experienced at Lakeside Camp reflect what happens in real life.

Suggestion(s) for extension

This is largely a whole-group activity with some work in mixed-ability groups, so that differentiation is largely by outcome. However, more able children can be encouraged to direct the freeze-frames in Session One and help their group make their caption attractive and/or amusing. Ask the children to think through the implications of any solutions put forward during the meetings in Session Two.

Suggestion(s) for support

Put less confident children in mixed-ability groups with those who will support and include them. Differentiation is largely by outcome but you can support the less confident during Session Two by joining in the mime work to help children with their tasks. Differentiate through questioning in the whole-group discussions.

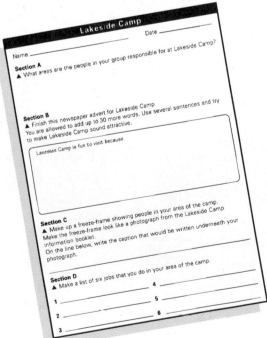

Assessment opportunities

Look for children who reveal a sense of audience by using persuasive images and language when composing their freeze-frames and captions. Note those children who can develop their own ideas and the ideas of others and those who can share relevant insights and opinions. Look for those who use appropriate dialogue when in role.

Opportunities for IT

Children could use a word processor to draft and redraft a list of rules for the campsite. As the activity progresses, the list could be extended or amended depending on the problems that arise and the solutions that are found. This would involve children in saving and retrieving their list of rules. The final list could be formatted to be presented as a poster to be displayed in a prominent position on the campsite. Encourage the children to discuss the style of writing and the intended audience for the rules.

The children could also use an art or drawing package to create a map of the campsite or to design posters to advertise the site.

Display ideas

Make a corner of the room into an information centre for Lakeside Camp. This can include the map, posters, leaflets, routes and paintings of the lake and other attractions. It could also include a three-dimensional model of the site.

Reference to photocopiable sheet

Photocopiable page 155 helps the children to invent details of their roles of responsibility in the drama and focuses on the need to attract the customers when building up a campsite business. This helps the children appreciate the need to solve any problems which could upset the customers or the neighbours in Session Two of the drama.

THE JUICY SWEET FACTORY

To build confidence in moving from sound and movement to improvisation.

👥 *Whole class and pairs.*

🕐 *45–60 minutes.*

Previous skills/knowledge needed

Children should know something about how sweets might be produced in a sweet factory and the different machines that might be used.

Key background information

In this activity children move from making machine movements and sounds to operating the machines in role as machine operators. Use the word 'Action' to start the activities each time and blow a whistle to stop them.

Preparation

Make a sign saying 'Juicy sweet factory'. Make one copy of photocopiable page 156 per pair of children.

Resources needed

A large space, photocopiable page 156, a piece of card, writing materials, a clipboard, a whistle.

What to do

Show the class the 'Juicy sweet factory' sign and ask the children to imagine that it is a real factory. Explain that the factory has been in business since 1924 and some of the machines are quite old. Talk about the kinds of machines that might be used to make the sweets and discuss what movements the machines might make, such as moving repetitively up and down or round and round. Talk about the shapes of the machines, such as round, long, twisted, tall and so on.

Put the children into pairs and tell t[h]
Ask them to work together to make
shape of a machine and then invent a
movement to accompany it. Encourage the childr[en]
as many different parts of their bodies as possible to represent different parts of their machine. After a while, stop the activity and let the class perform their machines to each other, half the class at a time.

Ask the class to stand in a large rectangular shape to represent the walls of the factory. Make sure the children are standing by their partners. Explain that in the next activity, you will ask them to be machine operators working on machines around the edges of the factory. Pairs will work on identical machines that are located next to each other.

Give each pair a copy of photocopiable page 156. Read through the sheet with the class to make sure everyone understands what to do and then ask the children to complete it. Make it clear that pairs should invent a sequence of simple movements that can be carried out in a small area around the edges of the factory walls. When pairs have worked out their movements, encourage them to discuss their instructions to check their clarity. Then ask them to stand in the rectangular shape as before and place their instruction sheets on the floor, between their two imaginary machines.

Tell the children to sit down where they are and then ask one pair to start their machine-operating movements. They should be joined by the next pair and the next and so on, until all the class are operating their machines. Then stop the movements and tell the class to sit down again. Repeat this until the children are confident.

Talk about some of the sounds that old factory machines might make and discuss how these can be made using their bodies and their voices, such as clapping, stamping

nd making steam-like sounds. Give each pair a few minutes to make up at least two machine sounds each, using their bodies and their voices. Emphasize that the sounds should be general sounds for the factory and not specifically for their own machines.

Explain that when you pull an imaginary lever in the factory, the power will move slowly to start each pair of machines in turn. The children should start off sitting on the floor. When you pull the lever, the first pair should stand up and start their sounds. They should keep their sounds going as the other pairs join them, one at a time. Explain that when you blow the whistle and pull the imaginary lever again, the power will cut off and they should stop making the sounds. Run through this activity once or twice, until the children seem confident.

Now tell the children that they must repeat the activity, but this time, when the final whistle blows they should stop making the sounds and start work on their machines.

Make it clear that workers are allowed to talk to each other as they work. Collect some suggestions about what the workers might talk about. Then run the sound and movement sequence and enter the factory as the supervisor. Ask pairs if they have any problems with their machines and if so, suggest that they check their instruction sheets and/or fetch some tools and try to fix the problem. Stop the drama after a few minutes by blowing the whistle twice and announcing a tea break.

Suggestion(s) for extension

Put more able children together and encourage them to make up the maximum eight movements for their sequence on the photocopiable sheet. Encourage them to experiment with different vocal sounds when making the sounds for the machines. Ask more able pairs to work out a sequence to combine the machine movements, sounds and machine-operator movements.

They should perform the sequence of movements they have written on their sheets. Allow them a few minutes to look at their sheets to remind themselves of the movements if necessary. Explain that two blows on the whistle will be used to end the movement sequence. Have a rehearsal and then perform it.

Tell the children that next time they run through the sound and movement sequence, you will pick up the clipboard and play the part of a factory supervisor. Explain that they should now play the parts of people who work the machines rather than the machines themselves. Tell them that, as the supervisor, you will come round to check things and talk to them as they work on their machines.

Suggestion(s) for support

Put less confident children together to work with an adult helper or with yourself when filling in the photocopiable sheets, or devise a simplified version involving drawing their machines. Ask them to concentrate on just one or two basic movements and sounds that they will be able to remember.

Assessment opportunities

Look for children who are imaginative and inventive in their choice of movements and sounds. Note those who can remember and repeat their sequences on cue. Check whether children have written clear instructions on their sheets.

DRAMA

Performance ideas

Groups can make up jingles advertising a brand of 'juicy sweet' and these can be recorded onto a cassette and played to the class. The sounds and movements can also be developed into a dance performance on the general theme of machines.

Reference to photocopiable sheet

Photocopiable page 156 provides a discussion and a language stimulus to help the children invent an appropriate movement sequence based on working a machine.

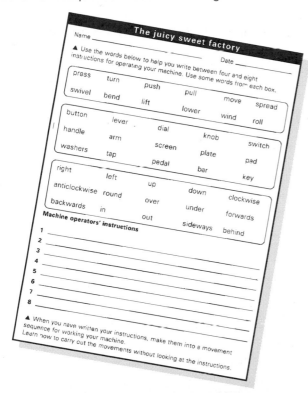

BE A NUMBER

To develop confidence in using physical theatre to represent two-dimensional shapes.

†† Whole class and pairs.

🕐 45 minutes.

Previous skills/knowledge needed

Children should be familiar with the layout of simple addition, subtraction and multiplication sums.

Key background information

This activity uses physical theatre to make numbers and simple sums, which can be more or less complicated depending on the needs of the class.

Preparation

Make one copy per child of photocopiable page 157. Write the numbers 0 to 9 on a large sheet of paper to make a number line and add the signs for plus, minus, multiply and

equals. Write out five to ten sums on another large sheet of paper. Make the second and subsequent sums incomplete: for example 7 – 4 = ☐; or 5 +☐= 7. Make sure that the room is suitable for movement activities and the children are appropriately dressed in soft shoes and loose clothing.

Resources needed

A large space, photocopiable page 157, two large sheets of paper, writing materials.

What to do

Begin by arranging the children in a semicircle. Show them the number line and ask if anyone can show the class how they might make the shape of the 0 using their body, either on the floor or upright. Repeat this with the rest of the numbers.

Give out copies of photocopiable page 157 and ask the children to try out their own versions of the numbers. Explain that there are no right ways of making the numbers, but if they need to they can refer to the pictures in section A on their sheet to give them some ideas. Suggest that they work in pairs to help each other. Each child can try to make a number on their own first, then they can work to produce some of the numbers as a pair, if they prefer.

As pairs finish, ask them to work out shapes for the numbers and sums on section B of the sheet. These include working as a pair to make the signs for add, subtract, multiply and equals. Call the children back into the semicircle and display the paper with the sums written on it. Ask some children to make the numbers and signs in order to represent the shapes of each sum, together with the missing numbers. Use two children to make numbers over 9. Then ask children to come out to the front and make any

Encourage the children to use copies of the photocopiable sheet to help them make the shapes of the numbers. Ask them to trace round their partner's body shape with their finger to see if it makes the shape of the number. Alternatively, let children make the shapes by lying on the floor and letting their partner draw a chalk mark around them to check for accuracy. For the movement sequence, put less confident children in small groups to work with an adult helper or put them in groups of three with children who will support them.

Assessment opportunities
Look for children who are confident in using their bodies to represent shapes and note those children who strive for accuracy. Look for children who support their partners and make suggestions to help them. Note those who use movements imaginatively to make an interesting sequence.

Performance ideas
The movement sequences can be developed and extended to make a number dance for a performance.

Display ideas
Children can dress in clothing of similar colour to perform a number of sums, which can then be photographed for a display.

Reference to photocopiable sheet
Photocopiable page 157 provides examples of how to make number shapes with the body. Less confident children can copy these shapes and others can refer to them or adapt them to invent their own versions.

number of their choice, without telling the class what it is. The class should guess. Other children can then build up the rest of the sum with their bodies. Let children choose their own numbers and decide where to place them in the sum. For example, the first child may make a number to represent the answer to a sum.

Now ask a child to make the 0 shape at the front of the class. Ask the class to suggest different ways in which this child can move from the 0 shape to make the number 1. These might include straightening up with a small jump, moving slowly into position, crumpling the 0 shape with wavy arm movements before straightening into the 1 shape. Encourage the class to think of as many ways of moving as possible and ask children to demonstrate their ideas.

Next, suggest that the child has a partner to work alongside him or her. The pair of children can carry out the same movements alongside each other or they can move in opposite ways, for example one moving quickly, one moving slowly. Talk about how the partners might move from a number 1 shape into a number 2 shape and let them demonstrate a few ideas.

Tell the class to work with their partners to make up a movement sequence, moving from one number to another from 0 to 10. The 10 will bring partners together to make one number with two digits. Encourage the children to make their movements flow and include as much variety of movement as possible. Finally, ask pairs of children to perform their sequences to the class in groups of six.

Suggestion(s) for extension
Ask the children to make two numbers and then let them move closer together to make a two-digit number. Suggest that they develop this by making up a dance sequence showing the two numbers making friends.

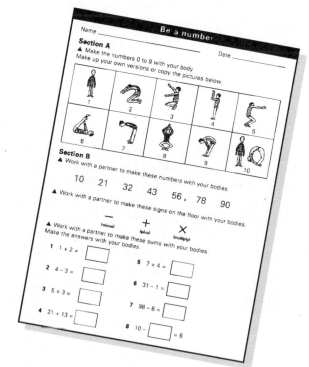

Photocopiables

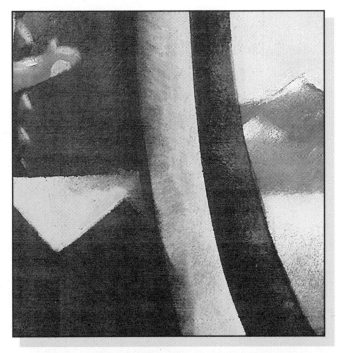

The pages in this section can be photocopied for use in the classroom or school which has purchased this book, and do not need to be declared in any return in respect of any photocopying licence.

They comprise a varied selection of both pupil and teacher resources, including pupil worksheets and resource material. All the photocopiable pages are related to individual activities in the book; the name of the activity is indicated at the top of the sheet, together with a page reference indicating where the lesson plan for that activity can be found.

Individual pages are discussed in detail within each lesson plan, accompanied by ideas for adaptation where appropriate – of course, each sheet can be adapted to suit your own needs and those of your class. Sheets can also be coloured, laminated, mounted onto card, enlarged and so on where appropriate.

Pupil worksheets have spaces provided for children's names and for noting the date on which each sheet was used. This means that, if so required, they can be included easily within any pupil assessment portfolio.

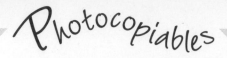

Punctuation line up, see page 14

Punctuation line up

Name _____   Date _____

▲ Read these sentences and add the missing punctuation.
Choose from these punctuation marks:

(.) full stop   (,) comma   (") speech marks

(?) question mark   (!) exclamation mark

1 Where are my jeans asked Becky

2 Come back here at once shouted the teacher

3 We are going to France for our school trip next year said Daniel

4 I like chocolate biscuits cream biscuits plain biscuits and all kinds of cake said Gemma

5 I feel really upset cried Sita as she picked up the broken toy

6 As Simon crossed the road Lucy yelled Watch out

7 When the door opened everyone shouted Surprise surprise

8 Can I have some carrots please asked Emma

▲ Work with a partner.
Make up a sound for each punctuation mark.
Look at the sentences and make sure you agree on the punctuation.
Now say each sentence, making a sound when you come to a punctuation mark.
Choose one of the sentences to demonstrate your punctuation sounds to the class.

▲ Make up some more sentences to perform and write them in the space below.

DRAMA

People meet people, see page 20

Radio script for 'People meet people'

Good morning ladies and gentlemen and welcome to **People meet people**, the radio show that brings people with different views face to face.
We have here today an invited audience, all of whom have strong views on the following issue: _____

(topic)

I have a list of questions, sent in by listeners, about this topic and I will now put them to the audience.
The **first** question is from Melissa of London who writes:

What do the audience think? Let's find out. Who would like to say something about Melissa's question?

The **second** question is from Robert of Glasgow who writes:

Would anyone like to say something about this?

The **third** question is from Kate of Wakefield who writes:

Does anyone have any strong opinions on this?

The **last** question is from a Mr Khan of Manchester who writes:

Who has something to say about this?

Time is running out, ladies and gentlemen, so let's ask those who haven't said very much so far for their views on this matter...
That's it. Thank you for listening. My thanks to the audience and those who wrote in. Join us next week for another exciting programme of **People meet people**. Goodbye.

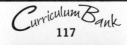

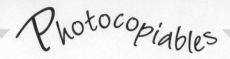

Audience profile for 'People meet people'

Name _____   Date _____

My name for the radio show is _____

My age is _____

My job or main interest is _____

_____

The town/village I live in is called _____

I have been invited on this programme because I feel strongly about the topic being discussed.

This is my strongest argument:

A class story, see page 22

Letter from Sam Harris, the radio storyteller

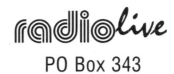

radiolive
PO Box 343

Dear Children

Please can you help me? My name is Sam Harris. I tell children's stories on Radio Live at 5 o'clock every Wednesday. I usually have a writer to make up the stories for me, but my writer has been taken ill and cannot provide me with a story for this week. When I asked the director of the radio station if she could find me another writer, she said there wouldn't be enough time to contact anyone. She told me to write this week's story myself. I am useless at making up stories for children. I don't know what to do.

This week's story is advertised as being about two children aged seven to eleven years old who go on a journey. I am writing to ask for your help because you will know the kind of stories children like to hear. I must have an outline of the story within the next 24 hours to meet the deadline for recording the programme. Can you think of a story and send me the outline, on paper or on an audio cassette, as soon as possible? If I use your story I will tell the listeners that it was yours. Thanking you in anticipation.

Best wishes from

Sam Harris

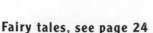 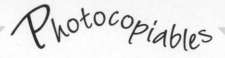

Fairy tales, see page 24

Narration for *Cinderella* (1)

CHARACTERS: Cinderella, two sisters, father, postman, fairy godmother, guests at the ball, prince, servant

(*Note:* Sections that are underlined are to be mimed.)

SCENE 1 Cinderella's kitchen

Once upon a time there was a girl called Cinderella who lived with her father and two stepsisters. Her stepsisters were very unkind to Cinderella and made her do all the work.
(*Enter Cinderella*) Cinderella had to sweep the floor, clean the windows, dust the furniture, cook the dinner and wash all her sisters' clothes.
(*Enter two sisters*) Every morning Cinderella's two sisters would come into the kitchen. They would shout at Cinderella and shake their fists until she brought them their breakfasts. They made fun of her all the time and laughed at her ragged clothes.
(*Enter father*) When Cinderella's father came into the kitchen for his breakfast, he didn't seem to notice what was happening. He just read his paper and ate his food.
Cinderella was always pleased when they finished their breakfast and left her in peace. (*Exit two sisters and father*)
At night Cinderella was often too busy to go to bed and would fall asleep in a chair in the kitchen.
One morning Cinderella was clearing away the breakfast things (*Enter postman*) when the postman called with a letter addressed to all the ladies in the house. Cinderella opened the letter and looked very sad.
The letter was an invitation to the prince's ball, but Cinderella had no dress to wear and no coach to take her to the palace. She knew that her sisters would be going without her. She went off to hang out the washing feeling very sad.
(*Exit Cinderella*)

SCENE 2 That same night in the kitchen

(*Enter Cinderella*) That night Cinderella came back into the kitchen feeling very tired. She sat down in a chair and stared at the floor.
Suddenly there was a flash (*Enter fairy godmother*) as Cinderella's fairy godmother appeared. She waved her wand and a coach appeared outside the window. She waved it again and Cinderella found herself dressed in a beautiful gown and glass slippers. Cinderella looked very happy because she knew she could now go to the ball.

Narration for *Cinderella* (2)

The fairy godmother <u>warned Cinderella</u> that the magic would wear off at 12 o'clock and so she must be home by then. Cinderella <u>thanked her fairy godmother and left for the ball</u>. *(Exit Cinderella and fairy godmother)*

SCENE 3 At the ball

(Enter guests) The ballroom was full of <u>people talking and laughing</u>. *(Enter sisters)* <u>The two sisters arrived, but no one spoke to them, so they stood in a corner by themselves</u>. *(Enter prince)* By the time the prince arrived the place was packed. <u>He looked around for a while and then</u> *(Enter Cinderella)* <u>he noticed Cinderella arrive and went over to talk to her. The sisters were jealous</u>. They didn't recognize Cinderella. <u>Cinderella spent all night talking and dancing with the prince</u> and forgot about the time. When the clock on the wall chimed 12 o'clock <u>Cinderella ran out of the room</u> before the magic turned her dress into rags *(Exit Cinderella)*. In her hurry to leave, <u>Cinderella lost one of her glass slippers and the prince picked it up. He was so upset that he left the ball, and everyone went home wondering who Cinderella could be</u> and where she had gone. *(Exit all)*

SCENE 4 The next day in Cinderella's house

The prince went all over the town to find the person who wore the glass slipper. He visited every house so that all the ladies could try on the slipper to see if it belonged to them. Cinderella's sisters waited for the prince to come to their house. *(Enter sisters)* <u>They sat on chairs and took off their shoes, ready to try on the slipper</u>. *(Enter prince and servant with slipper on a cushion)* When the prince and his servant came to Cinderella's house, <u>the sisters tried on the slipper, but it would not fit either of them. The prince asked if there were any other ladies in the house</u>. *(Enter Cinderella)* <u>At that moment Cinderella came into the room to start the cleaning. The prince asked her to try on the slipper and it fitted her perfectly</u>. He knew this was the mystery person he had met at the ball and <u>he asked her to marry him. Cinderella was so happy, but the sisters were furious and quickly left the room</u> *(Exit sisters)*. <u>Cinderella left to marry the prince</u> *(Exit Cinderella and prince and servant)* and they lived happily ever after.

Fairy tales, see page 24

A modern version of *Cinderella*

Name _____ Date _____

▲ Fill in your new list of characters if they are different from the usual story.

Cinderella
The two sisters
The father
The fairy godmother
The prince
The prince's servant
The ball
The glass slipper

▲ Choose **one** of the following scenes and write a modern version of it as if you are the narrator.

SCENE 1 In Cinderella's kitchen
Cinderella has to do all the work in the house. Her sisters are unkind to her. Her father ignores her. She is often so tired that she falls asleep in the kitchen.

SCENE 2 One morning in the kitchen
Cinderella receives an invitation to the ball. She is upset because she cannot go. Her fairy godmother gives her a coach, a dress and glass slippers. She must be home by 12 o'clock.

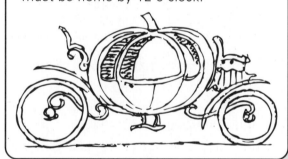

SCENE 3 At the ball
Cinderella dances with the prince. Her sisters do not recognize her. They are jealous. At 12 o'clock Cinderella runs away from the prince and drops her slipper. The prince picks it up.

SCENE 4 A room in Cinderella's house the next day
The prince and his servant arrive looking for the owner of the slipper. Every lady is asked to try it on. The sisters try on the slipper, but it doesn't fit them. Cinderella tries on the slipper. It fits perfectly and the prince asks her to marry him. She accepts and they live happily ever after.

DRAMA

The unfinished story, see page 26

The Elder's story

This is a true story – listen and you will know of the future.

Tonight will be a strange and special night, the like of which has never been seen before in this land. But first I must tell you of a secret happening in this place, which no one but the Elder could know.

Many years ago when the wall was first built, there was a door in the wall made of pure glass. The glass was so clear that you could see out for miles into the dangerous land beyond. The dangerous land looked very beautiful through the glass door, but the people of this village never dared to open it or walk through it, for fear of what would happen to them on the other side.

But one night one of our people came to me. This person talked of a dream they had dreamed the night before. This is what the person said:

'In my dream I walked out of the glass door into the dangerous land beyond. It was a land of peace and wonder, and in the distance I saw a castle made of pure glass like the door. Then I heard a voice inside me saying, 'Come to the castle of glass and you will be at peace for ever.'

I was scared and told the person to forget the dream. But that night, when everyone was asleep, the person walked silently through the door and was never seen again. The next morning the door was open and everyone was afraid. Fear crept through our hearts like icy fingers. I quickly ran to close the door and spoke to all the villagers. I forbade them to speak of this person ever again and made a rule that no one must ever go near the door. As the years have passed, the door has been covered with moss and people have forgotten about the door. But I have never forgotten. I have never forgotten.

Tonight, my friends, I must tell you this. Some time quite soon, the door will be opened again for the second time, but this time things will never be the same again.

When it happens you must leave this place, for it will no longer be a place of safety. Just remember that whatever happens, I care for you as much as you care for me. Remember my words: Our strength is as one. Remember these words. Remember these words.

Remember, remember, see page 32

Eyewitnesses (1)

▲ Try to tell the reporters everything you can remember about what you saw. Use the picture to help you. Invent more details about what you saw before and after the moment shown on the picture. Tell the reporters when you are ready to be interviewed.

You were here.

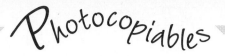

Remember, remember, see page 32

Eyewitnesses (2)

▲ Try to tell the reporters everything you can remember about what you saw. Use the picture to help you. Invent more details about what you saw before and after the moment shown on the picture. Tell the reporters when you are ready to be interviewed.

You were here.

DRAMA

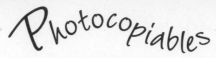

Journalists' questions

Name _____   Date _____

▲ Read through the questions on this sheet and use them as a guide when questioning the witnesses. Try to find out as much as you can about the crime. Make brief notes while the interview is taking place. (Write on the back of the sheet if you need to.)

1 What are your names and how old are you?

2 Where were you when you saw the crime?

3 Will each of you describe what you saw in as much detail as possible?

4 How many suspects did you see?
Please describe each of the suspects in as much detail as possible, for example: male or female? tall, medium height or short? fat, medium build or thin? colour of hair? clothing?

5 If there was a getaway vehicle, please describe it in as much detail as possible.

6 Were there any other witnesses? If so, who were they?

7 Describe how you felt when you saw the crime.

Script on tape, see page 38

Character sheet

Name _____   Date _____

The name of my character _____

1 What my character likes about the paintings

2 What my character does not like about the paintings

3 What my character feels about visiting the art gallery

DRAMA

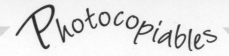

Can you mime it?, see page 42

Mime cards (1)

1   Taking a dog for a walk

Call the dog / Put the collar and lead on the dog / Walk the dog along the street / Go to a field and let the dog off the lead / Throw a ball for the dog to bring back / Put the lead back on the dog / Walk home / Open the back door with a key and go inside.

4   Getting ready to play sport

Walk into the changing room, carrying your kit in a bag / Put down the bag and take out your kit / Put on your kit / Do a warm-up exercise such as press-ups / Go to your bag and take out some coins / Go to a drinks machine and buy a drink / Drink the drink / Look round the room for a bin and put your empty can or cup into the bin / Pick up a ball and walk out ready to play.

2   Sending a letter

Find some paper, an envelope and a pen / Write the letter, but stop writing sometimes to think about what to write / Fold the letter, put it in the envelope and seal it / Address the envelope and put a stamp on it / Put on a coat / Pick up the letter and your door key / Leave the house and close the door / Walk to the postbox and post the letter / Walk home / Unlock the front door and go inside.

5   Washing a car

Fill a bucket with water and add some car shampoo / Put a sponge into the bucket of water / Carry the bucket to the car, squeeze out the sponge and wash the car / Find a hosepipe and connect it to the tap / Turn on the tap and hose down the car / Find a cloth and wipe the car dry / Carry the bucket to a sink or drain and empty it out / Sit inside the car and look pleased.

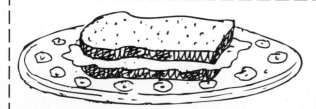

3   Making lunch

Put two slices of bread on a plate / Take some food from the fridge to make a sandwich / Get a knife from a drawer and make your sandwich / Make a drink / Open a packet of biscuits and put a few on a plate / Take a piece of fruit from a bowl and put this on the plate with the biscuits / Carry your lunch to the table / Eat your lunch.

6   Washing a big dog

Fill a large bath with water / Fetch some soap / Look for the dog who is hiding / Chase and catch the dog / Try to get the dog to get in the bath, but then push it in / Wash the dog with the soap / Rinse the dog by pouring water over it / The dog jumps out and shakes water all over you.

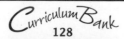

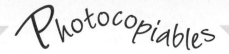

Can you mime it?, see page 42

Mime cards (2)

7 On the beach

Carry a towel to a place on the sand and sit on the towel / Take some suncream from your bag and put it on / Put the cream away and put on some sunglasses / Take a spade from your bag and build a sandcastle / Collect pebbles and shells to decorate your sandcastle / Go paddling in the sea / Dry your feet / Pack your bag and leave the beach.

10 Tidying a bedroom

Look at the mess and look fed up / Pick up some clothes from the floor and put them in a drawer or in a wardrobe / Pick up a magazine or a comic from the floor and start to read it / Throw the magazine or comic under the bed / Make the bedcovers look tidy / Find some bits of paper and throw them in the bin / Put some more things under the bed / Lie on the bed and go to sleep.

8 In the self service café

Find a tray and put it on the counter / Walk along and put a plate of sandwiches on your tray / Walk further on, then choose a cake to put on your tray / Get a drink from a machine / Find your money and pay for your food / Move through the crowded café to find an empty table / Sit down and take the things off your tray / Eat your food.

11 At the shoe shop

Look at your shoes and look unhappy / Look at some shoes in a shop window and then go inside / Take two shoes from a stand and sit down / Show them to the assistant / Wait for a moment and take off one of your shoes and try on one of the new ones / Walk around in the shoe as if it is too tight / Take off the shoe and try on both shoes of the other new pair / Walk around in them as if they fit well / Take off the shoes, put on your old shoes and take the new shoes in the box to the counter.

9 At the supermarket

Find a trolley and wheel it into the supermarket / Look along the shelves and take a tin of baked beans from the top shelf / Walk along and take a box of cereal from a bottom shelf / Go to the freezer section and choose some ice-cream / Walk to the checkout and load your shopping onto the counter / Walk to the end of the counter and put your shopping into bags / Find your money and pay the assistant / Wheel your trolley to the car and unload it into the boot.

12 At the cinema

Stand as if you are waiting in a cinema queue / Buy your tickets and then some popcorn / Walk into the cinema, undo your coat and sit down / Look at your watch and start to eat the popcorn / The first film is funny and makes you smile / The second film is a horror film and makes you look scared / Drop some of your popcorn on to the floor by mistake – look worried, but decide you'll have to leave it / When the films have finished, do up your coat and walk out slowly in a queue.

Mime a poem, see page 43

Mime words

Section A
▲ Work out actions for these words:

rain

house

funny

bright

flying

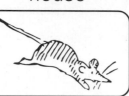
scurried

smoothly

cautiously

Section B
▲ Work out actions for the underlined words in these sentences.

1 My <u>dog</u> has a rubber <u>ball</u> that he <u>chews</u> on when he goes for a <u>walk</u>.

2 I <u>ran</u> <u>down</u> to the garden and saw a <u>large fish</u> <u>swimming</u> in the pond.

3 The <u>sun</u> was <u>high in the sky</u> as we <u>paddled</u> in the <u>sea</u>.

Section C
1 As we <u>crept cautiously</u> up the <u>winding path</u> towards the <u>door</u> of the <u>big house</u>, I suddenly began to feel very <u>cold</u> and <u>frightened</u>.

2 When the <u>football</u> went <u>through</u> the <u>window</u>, an <u>angry</u> <u>old man</u> came out of the <u>house</u>, <u>waving his fist</u>.

3 <u>Snow</u> fell <u>heavily</u>, as we <u>slowly climbed</u> the <u>hill</u> towards the <u>silent</u> <u>little</u> town.

Section D
1 The <u>stream</u> <u>glistened</u> in the <u>sunlight</u> and the <u>whispering</u> <u>trees</u> <u>swayed</u> like <u>dancers</u>, as we <u>sat</u> beneath them on the <u>grassy</u> bank.

2 She <u>switched off</u> the <u>computer</u> and <u>jumped up</u> to <u>look out</u> of the <u>open window</u>, just as the <u>postman</u> was <u>delivering</u> a <u>parcel</u> to the <u>house next door</u>.

3 We <u>waded</u> <u>through</u> the <u>squelching mud</u>, feeling <u>tired</u> and <u>exhausted</u>, as we tried to <u>reach</u> the <u>secret</u> <u>island</u> before nightfall.

DRAMA

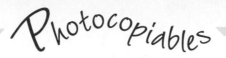

One minute on, see page 47

What's happening?

Name _____   Date _____

▲ What are the people in the picture thinking?
Fill in the thought bubbles.

▲ What might happen in the next minute?
Write some ideas below.

▲ Write a few sentences to describe what happened to the people
in your drama.

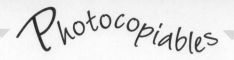

First lines

1   I like living here... I don't want to move!

- ✂ - -

2   It's not my fault... they're always picking on me!

- ✂ - -

3   I'm sorry... I didn't mean it!

- ✂ - -

4   Nobody in this house cares about me!

- ✂ - -

5   Everyone else is allowed to... so why can't I?

- ✂ - -

6   Can you lend me £5 for something really important?

- ✂ - -

7   I always knew this would happen!

- ✂ - -

8   Someone's got to tell the teacher about this!

- ✂ - -

9   Are you lost or are you looking for someone?

- ✂ - -

10 Have you heard what happened at dinner time?

Entrances, see page 50

30-second entrances

1 Children enter a kitchen looking for sweets that they have been told *not* to eat.

2 Burglars enter a house while the owner is asleep upstairs.

3 Children enter a room at 3 o'clock on Christmas morning to open their presents in secret, before they should.

4 An elderly person enters a carriage in a train to look for a lost umbrella. The passengers are trying to read or are looking out of the window.

5 A parent enters a messy house after a long day at work. The children have made all the mess and are hiding behind the settee.

6 People enter a newly opened gym to start a fitness session on the equipment.

7 A babysitter enters a bedroom to check on the children who are pretending to be asleep. The children play secretly after the babysitter has gone, but the babysitter keeps returning to check on them.

8 Strangers sit down at a table in a supermarket café and eat their food in silence. The table is too small.

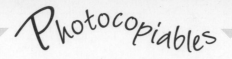

Advert planning sheet

Name _____   Date _____

Ideas for the advert	The best idea

Characters in the advert and who will play them
(Choose at least one character for each member of your group.)

1 _____

2 _____

3 _____

4 _____

▲ How will your advert start?

▲ How will your advert end?

▲ What persuasive words will you use?

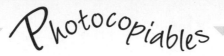

Acting in the school play, see page 54

Rehearsal grid

Date and time	Place	Rehearsal unit No.	Characters needed

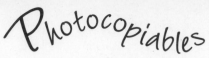
Acting in the school play, see page 54

Character profile

Name _____   Date _____

Section A

▲ Fill in these details about your character.

Name   Age

Where does your character live?

Who does your character like the most in the play?

Who does your character dislike the most in the play?

Describe your character's personality.

Section B

Which characters in the play like your character?	Which characters in the play do not like your character?

DRAMA

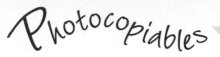
Critical review

Name of play

Name of theatre or theatre group

Date the play was seen

What part of the play did you like best and why?

What part of the play did you like least and why?

Did the audience seem to enjoy the whole play, parts of the play or none of the play?

Which character did you think was the best actor?

What did you like or dislike about the set?

What was your favourite costume and why did you like it?

If props were used, name some of the ones you noticed.

Did the play keep you interested all the time, some of the time or none of the time?

Describe any parts in the play that made you want to know what happened next.

Describe any parts in the play that made you feel happy, sad or angry.

Describe any parts in the play that made you think.

Would you recommend this play to a friend? Say why.

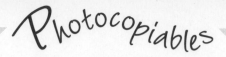

The jury, see page 62

What do you think?

Name _____ Date _____

Section A

My name is Jo and I live with my parents and my elder sister, Amy. My parents own a newsagent's shop. Amy and I sometimes work in the shop to give Mum and Dad a break. A few months ago my mum noticed that small things were going missing from the shop. At first it was just sweets, then later some cans of pop went missing and then magazines and videos began to disappear. My dad said he was going to call the police.

One night Amy went to her friend's house and I went into her room to borrow a tape. I found a box in her room containing some of the missing videos and several packets of sweets. When she came home I told her what I had found. She told me that I had no right to go into her room. Then she said that taking the things wasn't really stealing because they belonged to Mum and Dad. I didn't want to get her into trouble and so I agreed to say nothing.

A week later, a teacher saw her giving videos to people at school and now everyone says she is a thief. Did I do the right thing by keeping quiet?

Section B

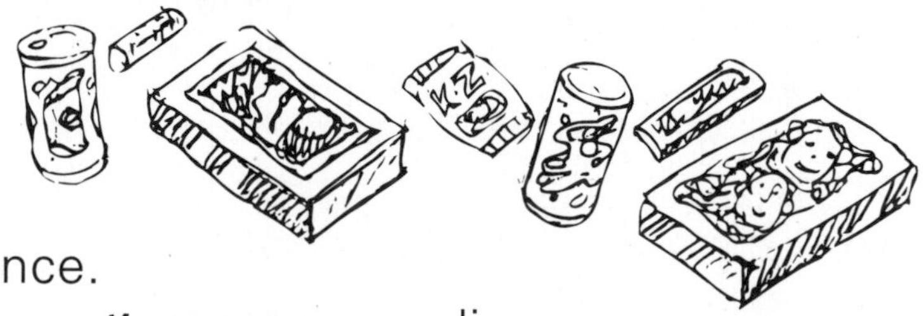

▲ What do you think?

Put a mark after each sentence.
✓ means you agree   ✗ means you disagree
? means you are unsure

1 Amy was only being kind to her friends and should not be called a thief.

2 Jo's mum and dad shouldn't have let their children work alone in the shop.

3 Taking things from your family without asking is stealing.

4 Jo's mum and dad should report Amy to the police, to teach her a lesson.

5 Jo should have asked Amy if she was being bullied into taking things.

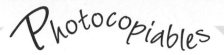

Censoring the media, see page 63

The horror video

Name _____   Date _____

▲ Read what happened in this house.

Craig is nineteen years old and is babysitting for Jack and Kirsty. Jack is seven years old and Kirsty is ten years old. Craig has bought a horror video to watch. He doesn't want Jack and Kirsty to watch it with him. They have an argument. Kirsty says that she should watch it and not Jack. Jack says that he should be allowed to watch it.

▲ Write down some of their arguments.

I'm Craig… and this is why I think that Jack and Kirsty should *not* watch the video.

I'm Kirsty… and this is why I think I should be allowed to watch the video.

I'm Jack… and this is why I think I should be allowed to watch the video.

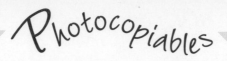

Thinking about bullying

Name _____   Date _____

▲ Which of the following is an example of bullying? Write either **Yes** or **No** in the box next to each sentence. Talk about each example with your partner first. You do not have to agree with your partner. There are no right or wrong answers.

1 Hanif knocks Ben's pencil case on the floor every time he walks past Ben's table at school.

2 Natalie and Sarah used to be friends with Lucy. Now they will not play with her.

3 James keeps calling Richard names like 'shorty' and 'titch' because Richard is the smallest in the class.

4 Every time Michael passes Emma, he pulls her hair.

5 Lee keeps tripping Matthew up in the playground.

6 Kate keeps following Hannah round at dinner time, trying to copy everything she does.

7 When Helen found out that Geeta was scared of spiders, she put a spider on Geeta's hair.

8 When the older children play football at playtimes, they use the whole playground and push the younger children out of the way.

9 A group of girls make fun of a boy who can't speak properly because he is deaf.

10 Andrew keeps pushing Christopher to the back of the dinner queue.

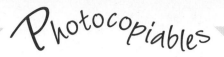

Friends and enemies, see page 69

Friends and enemies

Name _____   Date _____

▲ Look at the images below. Some show friendship and some show hatred. Write the word **friendship** or the word **hatred** under each image to show which is which.

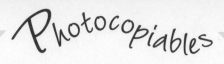

World of health and fitness, see page 71

World of health and fitness

Name ______________________________ Date ________________

Section A: Staff job description

Names of team: ______________________________

____

Details of main responsibilities:

Before opening

During opening hours

After closing

Section B: Job evaluation

What does your team like best about the work you do?

What does your team like least about the work you do?

What changes would you like to see happen, to improve your working day?

Not like us, see page 74

Volcano Island

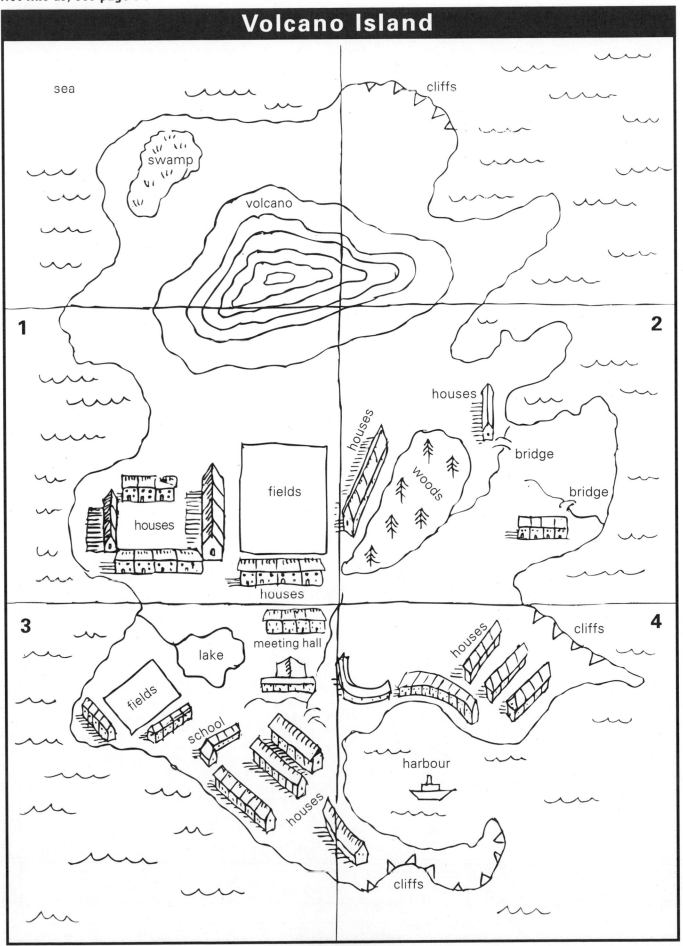

sea

cliffs

swamp

volcano

1

2

houses

houses

bridge

woods

bridge

fields

houses

houses

houses

3

4

cliffs

meeting hall

lake

houses

fields

school

houses

harbour

houses

cliffs

DRAMA

North Shern letter

Shern Town Hall
North Shern
SHERN ISLAND

Dear Volcano Islanders

In response to your request for help, we make the following invitation. We are very sorry to hear of the possible eruption of the volcano and we are pleased to say that we can offer you a place to stay and interesting work to do, here on the island of Shern.

　　We offer you work so that you can earn money to pay for your keep while you stay here, and perhaps you will be able to save some money towards rebuilding your homes if they are destroyed by the volcano.

　　You will be able to stay in one of our new hotels which offers comfortable rooms and the free use of the hotel swimming pool and bar. All your meals will be cooked for you at the hotel.

　　We have arranged for one of our officials to meet you at North Shern harbour boatyard when you arrive on your boats. We look forward to meeting you and will discuss what work you will do after you have settled into your hotel.

Yours sincerely

Shern Town Council

South Shern letter

South Shern
Residents' Association
South Shern Community Centre
South Shern
SHERN ISLAND

Dear Volcano Islanders

We, the people of South Shern, would like to apologize for the behaviour of our neighbours in North Shern. We cannot believe that they have set you to work in an old factory building and have made you stay in a boathouse. The people of North Shern are not like us. We would like to welcome you to our island and invite you to a welcome party next Saturday at South Shern Community Centre, which is a few miles from where you are staying. If you let us know how many of you will be coming, we will send buses for you at 7 o'clock.

Please accept our invitation of friendship. Send your reply by letter as soon as possible.

Yours sincerely

The residents of South Shern

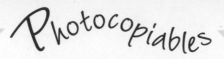

Circus, see page 78

What's in a circus?

Name _____   Date _____

▲ What do most people expect to see at a circus?
Join up each item to the box that you think is correct.
The first one has been done for you.

1   Supermarket

2   Lions and/or tigers

3   Clowns

4   Horses

5   Elephants   YES

6   Restaurant

7   Trapeze artists

8   Acrobats

9   Monkeys or chimpanzees

10 Sea lions   MAYBE

11 Dolphins

12 Knife throwers

13 Dogs

14 Jugglers

15 Tightrope walkers   NO

16 Parrots

17 Singers

18 Magician

19 Hairdresser

20 Fire-eaters and/or flame throwers

Brown's Circus

Dear Brown's Circus

I am disappointed that you have no animals in your circus and I feel that you have no right to call yourself a circus at all. Circuses have been around for many years and they always have acts that feature animals. You are deceiving the general public and should be reported to the police! I for one shall not come to see your so-called circus and I shall tell all my friends to keep away. I have also written to the newspapers.

From an angry circus lover

- ✂ - -

Dear Brown's Circus

I have just bought some tickets for your circus because my children love animals and are keen to see them perform tricks. We are disappointed to find that you do not include very many. We expected a circus to have large numbers of acts featuring animals and we don't think it's right that you should call yourself a real circus. I intend to hand back my tickets as a protest and will be contacting the newspapers to complain.

From a disappointed parent

- ✂ - -

Dear Brown's Circus

Why are you using animals in your circus? How can you be so cruel as to keep them caged up? They should be left in the wild where they belong. Even domestic animals should not be made to perform degrading tricks. They didn't choose to work with you. I shall be writing to the newspapers about this. Surely you can find other entertaining acts without exploiting poor animals.

From an animal lover

- ✂ - -

New settlers, see page 82

Instructions to new planet settlers

Name _____ Date _____

▲ Choose the most important things you will need to take with you to the new planet. You will be allowed to choose ten things from this list. Underline the ones you want to take and then pack them up carefully in bags and boxes.

▲ In addition to the items on this list, you will be allowed to take one small bag each for your own personal possessions. Label your bags and equipment and then take everything to the central collection point as soon as possible.

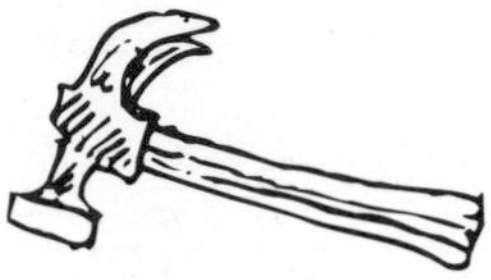

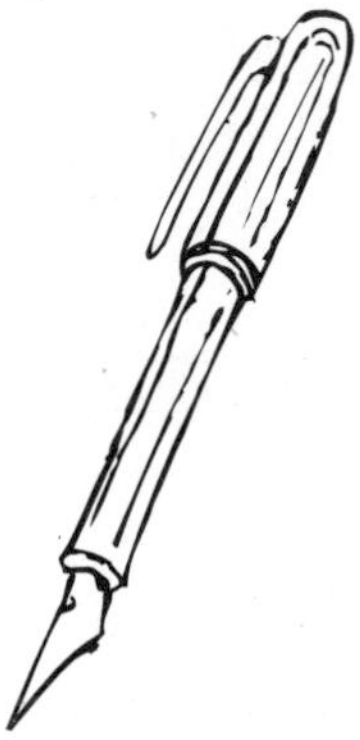

List of provisions and equipment

small tools for farming, building, carpentry

blankets

cutlery and crockery

a month's food supply

water carriers and buckets

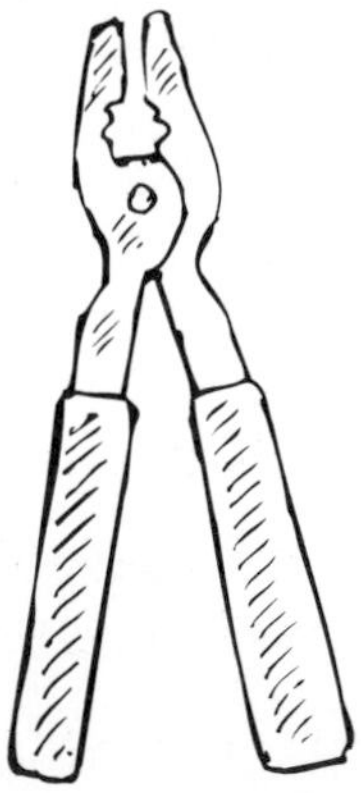

tents and camping equipment

matches

warm clothes, a sewing box and material

first aid kit and medical books

seeds for growing fruit and vegetables

small pieces of wood and metal

knives and scissors

pans and cooking utensils

paper and pens

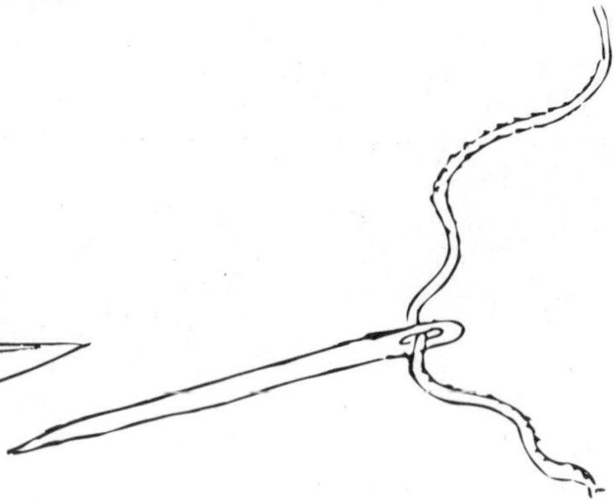

Historical village, see page 88

Villager's role sheet

Name _____   Date _____

▲ Fill in the spaces.
In the drama I will play the part of someone called _____

Here are some details about my role:
I live in a village and my occupation is _____

My family consists of _____

For my main meal I eat _____

I sleep on _____

If I have any free time I like to _____

_____

Here is a list of five jobs I do every day:

1 _____   **4** _____

2 _____   **5** _____

3 _____

The job I **enjoy** most is _____

The job I **dislike** most is _____

Here is a picture of me at work.   Here is a picture of where I live.

DRAMA

Tutankhamun, see page 91

Tutankhamun

Name _____ Date _____

▲ Fill in the archaeologist's thoughts in the bubbles.

Nov 1922 Today we started to look for the missing tomb of Tutankhamun.

We found 16 steps leading to a door. We had to wait for Lord Carnarvon to arrive!

▲ Draw the picture.

We found some beautiful objects in the chamber and took them to our tents.

▲ Fill in the thought bubbles.

The press and tourists crowded round the entrance to the tomb.

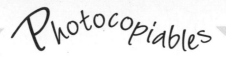

Theseus and the Minotaur, see page 95

Theseus and the Minotaur

Name _____ Date _____

▲ Fill in the missing words in these sentences about Theseus and the Minotaur.

1 Theseus sailed to Crete in a ship with a _____ (white, red, black) sail.

2 The Minotaur was half man and half _____ (fox, bull, dragon).

3 The Minotaur lived in a _____ (cave, labyrinth, castle).

4 Princess Ariadne gave Theseus a sword and some _____ (thread, food, water).

5 Theseus left Princess Ariadne on _____ (an iceberg, a mountain, an island).

6 On the way home, Theseus forgot to change _____ (his socks, the ship's sail).

7 Theseus' father threw himself off a _____ (building, cliff, tower).

▲ Who should we blame for the death of Aegeus (Theseus' father)? Read the list below and tick those you think are to blame.

1 The person who murdered King Minos' son at the Athenian games
2 King Minos
3 The Minotaur
4 Theseus
5 The young people who sailed with Theseus
6 Princess Ariadne
7 King Aegeus himself

▲ Tell your partner the reasons for your answers and listen to his or her opinions.

DRAMA

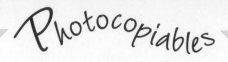
Pride of place

Name _____   Date _____

▲ Circle the facilities that are available in your local area.

health centre	dentist	hairdresser
supermarket	lake or river	seashore
sports centre	swimming pool	small shops
post office	library	school
telephone box	bus stop	children's park
railway station	café	restaurant

▲ Tick the statements that apply to your area.

1 Most people are friendly.
2 The countryside around here is beautiful.
3 Most people keep themselves to themselves.
4 Children have nowhere to play.
5 The area is usually clean and free of litter.
6 Some parts of the area are full of litter.
7 There is very little vandalism here.
8 The streets are quiet and peaceful in the evenings.
9 Children here are mostly well-behaved when they are out.
10 This is a busy area and young people have lots to do.
11 You can always find a shop open somewhere in the area.
12 You can get a bus or a train easily.

▲ What are the **two** best things about your area? Say why you
have chosen these things.

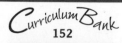

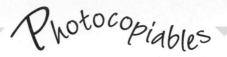

Oakton Theme Park, see page 102

Oakton village

Name _____   Date _____

new housing estate
old housing estate
farmland
Oakton Rd
shops
village green
pond
tree

school
hall
To Newbry
woods
cottages
Oakton Hall
lake
stream

▲ Fill in this questionnaire as if you were someone who lives in the village of Oakton.

Name _____   Age _____

Do you live on the new housing estate, on the old housing estate or in one

of the cottages? _____

How long have you lived in Oakton? _____

Do you have a job? _____

If you have a job, please explain what you do. _____

_____

Do you travel by car? _____

How do you spend your free time? _____

_____

_____

What do you like **best** about living in Oakton? _____

_____

_____

What do you like **least** about living in Oakton? _____

_____

_____

DRAMA

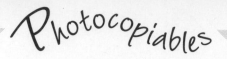
Oakton village and theme park proposal

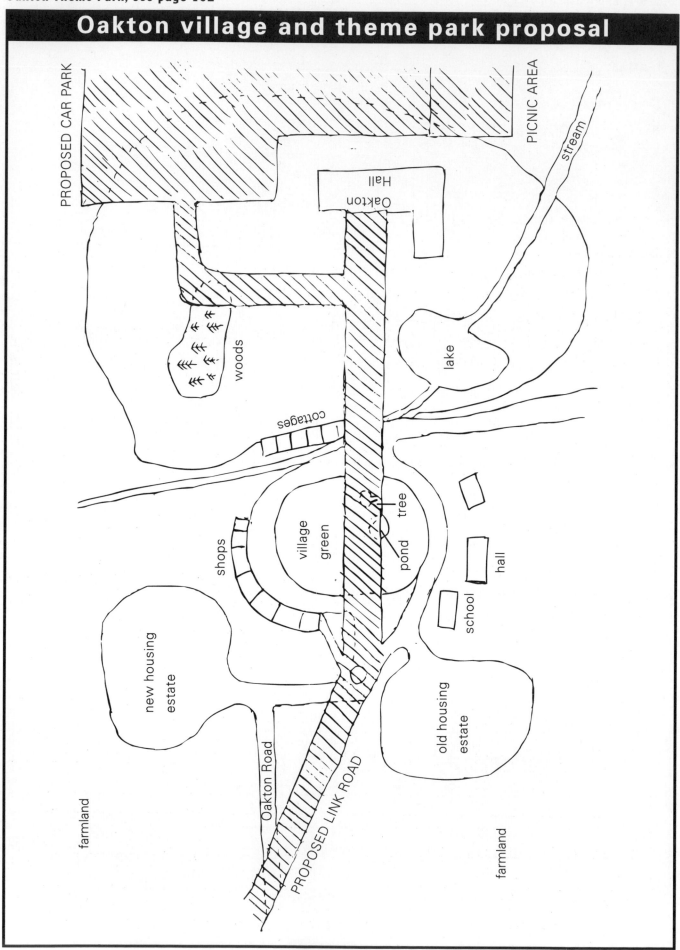

PROPOSED CAR PARK

PICNIC AREA

stream

Oakton Hall

woods

lake

cottages

village green

shops

pond

tree

hall

school

new housing estate

old housing estate

Oakton Road

PROPOSED LINK ROAD

farmland

farmland

Lakeside Camp, see page 108

Lakeside Camp

Name _____   Date _____

Section A
▲ What areas are the people in your group responsible for at Lakeside Camp?

Section B
▲ Finish this newspaper advert for Lakeside Camp.
You are allowed to add up to 30 more words. Use several sentences and try to make Lakeside Camp sound attractive.

> Lakeside Camp is fun to visit because

Section C
▲ Make up a freeze-frame showing people in your area of the camp.
Make the freeze-frame look like a photograph from the Lakeside Camp information booklet.
On the line below, write the caption that would be written underneath your photograph.

_____

Section D
▲ Make a list of six jobs that you do in your area of the camp.

1 _____   4 _____

2 _____   5 _____

3 _____   6 _____

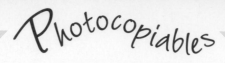

The juicy sweet factory, see page 111

The juicy sweet factory

Name _____   Date _____

▲ Use the words below to help you write between four and eight instructions for operating your machine. Use some words from each box.

press	turn	push	pull	move	spread
swivel	bend	lift	lower	wind	roll

button	lever	dial	knob	switch
handle	arm	screen	plate	pad
washers	tap	pedal	bar	key

right	left	up	down	clockwise
anticlockwise	round	over	under	forwards
backwards	in	out	sideways	behind

Machine operators' instructions

1 _____
2 _____
3 _____
4 _____
5 _____
6 _____
7 _____
8 _____

▲ When you have written your instructions, make them into a movement sequence for working your machine.
Learn how to carry out the movements without looking at the instructions.

Be a number, see page 113

Be a number

Name _____   Date _____

Section A
▲ Make the numbers 0 to 9 with your body.
Make up your own versions or copy the pictures below.

| 1 | 2 | 3 | 4 | 5 |
| 6 | 7 | 8 | 9 | 10 |

Section B
▲ Work with a partner to make these numbers with your bodies.

10   21   32   43   56   78   90

▲ Work with a partner to make these signs on the floor with your bodies.

−   +   ×

(minus)   (plus)   (multiply)

▲ Work with a partner to make these sums with your bodies.
Make the answers with your bodies.

1 1 + 2 = ☐   **5** 7 × 4 = ☐

2 4 − 3 = ☐   **6** 31 − 1 = ☐

3 5 × 3 = ☐   **7** 98 − 8 = ☐

4 21 + 13 = ☐   **8** 10 − ☐ = 6

DRAMA

INFORMATION TECHNOLOGY WITHIN DRAMA

Main IT Focus

The information technology activities outlined in this book can be used to develop and assess children's IT capability as outlined in the National Curriculum. The main emphasis for the development of IT capability within these activities is on communicating information. As many of the activities use the idea of freezing actions as a photograph or video, this section explores some of those related to Information and Communications Technologies (ICT) issues in more detail.

Using pictures from other sources

In many of the activities, pictures are used to record freeze-frames. Although these are representative of the children's work they could be recorded and used in other ICT-based activities in a number of different ways.

Many schools regularly use a traditional camera to take photographs or activities in school. With the advent of cheap flat-bed scanners, schools are able to turn these conventional photographs into digital images which can be used in a range of different applications. Modern scanners produce high-quality results at the best resolutions, but the files created can be very large. Schools need to experiment to find a resolution which creates good, usable images at the lowest memory requirement. Around 200 dpi is a good starting-point. This is especially important when schools are developing their own World Wide Web pages as large files take a long time to download.

An alternative approach to conventional photography is to use a digital camera. These cameras create digital images which can be transferred to a computer used in other software. They are easy to use and because there are no film or developing costs they can be a very cheap alternative to traditional photography for curriculum use. One particularly useful feature is the ability to look at the picture as soon as you have taken it. If you don't like it you can try again!

Many schools already have video cameras, and it is possible to select single images from a video camera and use them within other ICT applications. To achieve this you need a digitizer card or box which turns the video pictures into a digital format. It is also possible to digitize small video-clips and use them in multimedia presentations or World Wide Web pages. With the advent of the digital video camera which links directly to a computer, it has become even easier to use video-clips within such presentations. However, such files can be very large and need to be compressed using special software to make them usable.

Multimedia authoring software

This software is proving to be a very versatile and powerful medium for children of all ages. It combines many of the features of a word processor or desktop publishing package but its main difference is that the different pages of a child's work can be linked together. Depending on the way that the links are created, children can move to different parts of the presentation by simply clicking with a mouse on a symbol, word or picture. Such presentations usually begin with a title page which allows the user to move to different sections of a presentation.

The other important feature is the software's ability to handle a range of different information including text; pictures from art and drawing packages, scanned images and digital cameras; sounds from audio CDs or sound samples; and even moving pictures taken from a CD-ROM or captured using a video camera. Some of these latter areas require specialized equipment but the mixing of text, pictures and simple recorded sounds can be undertaken with the minimal amount of equipment. The data files created by such work can be very large and a computer with a hard disk and large memory is needed. If the final presentation is to be moved to other computers via a floppy disk, this will also limit the number of pages and amount of pictures and sound-clips that can be included.

Work with authoring packages is best undertaken as a part of a longer project, with children working collaboratively in groups. A class presentation can be split among several groups, with each one preparing the text and pictures for their section and deciding how the pages are to be laid out and linked. Children will need support when they first start to put their ideas into the computer. They will need to know how to create frames, alter text styles, add colours, import graphics and sound files from other disks and make the links between pages. A class structure can be set up in advance which gives a starting-point for group work. It is a good idea for the teacher to spend some time with the software before embarking on a project with the children.

As the National Grid for Learning (NGFL) develops, children will begin to publish their own resources, or World Wide Web pages, which are a similar form of multimedia presentation. World Wide Web pages are written in a special format called HTML. Pages can contain text, sounds, still and moving pictures. A number of primary word processors are now able to create www pages in HTML format and allow children to link them together to create simple sequences of linked pages. The school will be able to save these to a hard drive, make them accessible across a school network, add them to an LEA Intranet or even publish them as a part of the school's website.

The grids on the opposite page relate the activities in this book to specific areas of IT and to relevant software resources. Types of software rather than names of specific

programs have been listed to enable teachers to use the ideas regardless of the computers to which they have access. The software should be available from most good educational software retailers. Teachers may wish to include specific software which addresses the content and understanding of the topics being taught. Activities are referenced by page number (bold page numbers indicate activities which have expanded IT content).

AREA OF IT	SOFTWARE	ACTIVITIES (PAGE NOS.)			
		CHAPTER 1	**CHAPTER 2**	**CHAPTER 3**	**CHAPTER 4**
Communicating Information	Word processor	**16**, 18, 22, 24, 34	38, 45, 58	65, 67, 74, 78, 82, 84	88, 91, **100**, **102**, 108
Communicating Information	Desktop publishing	**16**, 22		67, 71, 74	91
Communicating Information	Art package	22, 24	38, 52	71, 78	102, 108
Communicating Information	Drawing software	18	52	71	102, 108
Communicating Information	Authoring software	18, **29**			**100**
Information handling	NGFL		47, 52	74, 82	88, **91**, 98
Information handling	Database		58	78	
Information handling	CD-ROMs		47	74, 82	88, **91**, 98
Control	Digital/video camera	18, 20, 29	45		**100**
Modelling	Simulation				91

SOFTWARE TYPE	BBC/MASTER	RISCOS	NIMBUS/186	WINDOWS	MACINTOSH
Word processor	Folio	Pendown Desk Top Folio Textease	All Write Write On	Word Write Away Textease ClarisWorks	Word EasyWorks ClarisWorks Creative Writer
Desktop publishing		Pendown DTP Ovation Textease		PagePlus Publisher Textease	
Art package	Picture Builder	1st Paint Kid Pix Dazzle	Picture Builder	Colour Magic Kid Pix 2 Microsoft Paint	Kid Pix 2 Microsoft Paint ClarisWorks
Drawing software		Draw Vector Art Works	Picture Builder	Dazzle ClarisWorks Oak Draw Genesis	
Multimedia authoring		Magpie Hyperstudio Genesis Textease		Hyperstudio Illuminatus Textease	Hyperstudio
Drawing package	Picture Builder Grass	Draw Picture IT Art Works		ClarisWorks Microsoft Draw Sparks	ClarisWorks Microsoft Draw
Database		Junior Pinpoint Junior Find IT Key Note	Grass	Junior Find IT Information Workshop	ClarisWorks EasyWorks

DRAMA

	MATHS	SCIENCE	HISTORY	GEOGRAPHY	D&T	IT	ART	MUSIC	RE	PE
LANGUAGE AND LITERACY		Choosing plants for a commemorative garden.	Depicting moments from the past.	Debating environmental issues.		Recording sounds for punctuation onto an audio cassette. Using word processor to write scripts. Using video and digital cameras.	Drawing pictures to record significant moments. Designing and depicting a commemorative garden.		Depicting moments from stories. Thinking about communities and leaders.	Physical theatre.
THEATRE SKILLS	Timing performances.				Designing and making props. Designing and making books of plays.	Reading and recording scripts onto an audio cassette. Using word processor to write scripts and theatre reviews.	Looking at famous paintings and reading about the artists. Depicting freeze-frames or photographs.	Using percussion to perform adverts.	Thinking about how people express feelings verbally and non-verbally.	Linking mime with movement.
PERSONAL AND SOCIAL DEVELOPMENT		Researching information on health and fitness. Looking at space travel.	Thinking about the origins of using animals in a circus.	Researching volcanic eruptions and the effects on inhabitants. Looking at a map of a volcanic island.		Reading and recording scripts onto an audio cassette. Drafting letters and making leaflets on a word processor. Using a camera.	Sketching freeze-frames for a magazine illustration. Using clip art to produce leaflets and posters.	Selecting or creating music for a ceremony.	Considering moral dilemmas and issues. Looking at community rules, for example the Ten Commandments.	Looking at health and fitness amenities for the public. Physical theatre.
CROSS-CURRICULAR THEMES	Working out sums.	Thinking about the forces and movements of factory machines.	Working in role as part of a community in the past. Researching background information to historical events and myths.	Reading maps. Discussing local amenities. Considering environmental issues. Looking at leisure facilities.	Designing and making a 3D model of a campsite.	Using CD-ROM for research. Using a digital camera. Using a desktop publishing package.	Making brochures, posters and painting scenes for information and persuasion.	Making sound effects for machines.		Dance drama about building a Roman road. Making machine movements.